A-Z SW

CW00343732

CONT

REFERENCE

Motorway	M4	Church or Chapel	†
A Road	A419	Cycleway (selected)	
Under Construction		Fire Station	■
B Road	B4534	Hospital	🄗
Dual Carriageway		House Numbers (A & B Roads only)	68 1
One-way Street	→	Information Centre	🄸
Traffic flow on A Roads is also indicated by a heavy line on the driver's left.	→	National Grid Reference	⁴10
Restricted Access		Park & Ride Wroughton	P+
Pedestrianized Road		Police Station	▲
Track & Footpath		Post Office	★
Residential Walkway	⋯⋯	Safety Camera with Speed Limit	(30)
Railway	Heritage Station / Station / Level Crossing	Fixed cameras and long term road works cameras Symbols do not indicate camera direction	
Built-up Area	UNION ST.	Toilet:	
		without facilities for the Disabled	▽
		with facilities for the Disabled	▽
Local Authority Boundary	— ∙ — ∙ —	Educational Establishment	▭
Posttown Boundary		Hospital or Healthcare Building	▭
Postcode Boundary (within Posttown)	— — —	Industrial Building	▭
		Leisure or Recreational Facility	▭
Map Continuation	10 Large Scale Town Centre 5	Place of Interest	▭
		Public Building	▭
		Shopping Centre or Market	▭
Car Park (selected)	P	Other Selected Buildings	▭

SCALE

Map Pages 6-37 1:15,840	Map Pages 4-5 1:7,920
4 inches (10.16cm) to 1 mile 6.31cm to 1 km	8 inches (20.32cm) to 1 mile 12.63cm to 1 km
0 ¼ ½ Mile	0 ⅛ ¼ Mile
0 250 500 750 Metres	0 100 200 300 Metres

Copyright of Geographers' A-Z Map Company Limited

Fairfield Road, Borough Green, Sevenoaks, Kent TN15 8PP
Telephone: 01732 781000 (Enquiries & Trade Sales)
01732 783422 (Retail Sales)
www.a-zmaps.co.uk
Copyright © Geographers' A-Z Map Co. Ltd.
Edition 5 2009

Ordnance Survey® This product includes mapping data licensed from Ordnance Survey® with the permission of the Controller of Her Majesty's Stationery Office.
© Crown Copyright 2008. All rights reserved. Licence number 100017302
Safety camera information supplied by www.PocketGPSWorld.com
Speed Camera Location Database Copyright 2008 © PocketGPSWorld.com

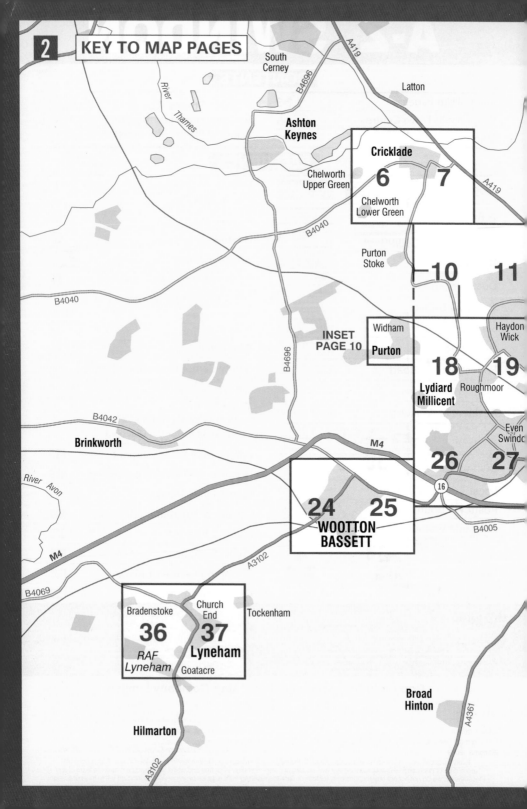

South Cerney

Latton

A419

River Thames

B4696

Ashton Keynes

Chelworth Upper Green

Cricklade

6 **7**

Chelworth Lower Green

A419

B4040

Purton Stoke

10 **11**

B4040

B4696

Widham

INSET PAGE 10

Purton

Haydon Wick

18 **19**

Lydiard Millicent Roughmoor

B4042

M4

Brinkworth

Even Swindo

River Avon

26 **27**

24 **25**

WOOTTON BASSETT

16

B4005

M4

B4069

A3102

Bradenstoke

Church End

Tockenham

36 **37**

RAF Lyneham **Lyneham**

Goatacre

Broad Hinton

A4361

Hilmarton

A3102

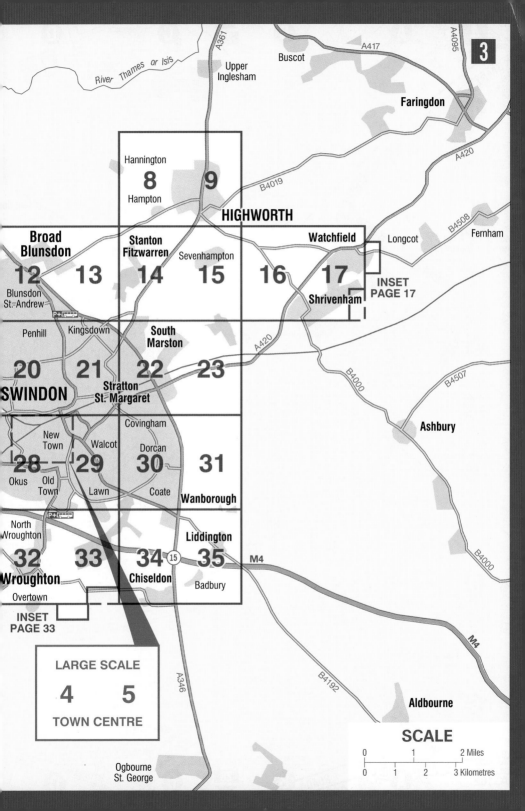

3

River Thames or Isis

Upper Inglesham

Buscot

A417

A4095

A361

Faringdon

A420

B4019

Hannington

8   **9**

Hampton

HIGHWORTH

B4508   Fernham

Watchfield   Longcot

Broad Blunsdon

12   **13**

Blunsdon St. Andrew

Stanton Fitzwarren

14

Sevenhampton

15

16   **17**

Shrivenham

INSET PAGE 17

P+

Penhill   Kingsdown

South Marston

A420

B4000

B4507

20   **21**   **22**   **23**

SWINDON

Stratton St. Margaret

Ashbury

Covingham

New Town   Walcot

Dorcan

28   **29**   **30**   **31**

Okus   Old Town

Lawn   Coate

Wanborough

B4000

P+

North Wroughton

Liddington

32   **33**   **34** 15 **35**   M4

Wroughton   **Chiseldon**

Overtown   Badbury

INSET PAGE 33

M4

LARGE SCALE

4   **5**

TOWN CENTRE

A346

B4192

Aldbourne

Ogbourne St. George

SCALE

0   1   2 Miles

0   1   2   3 Kilometres

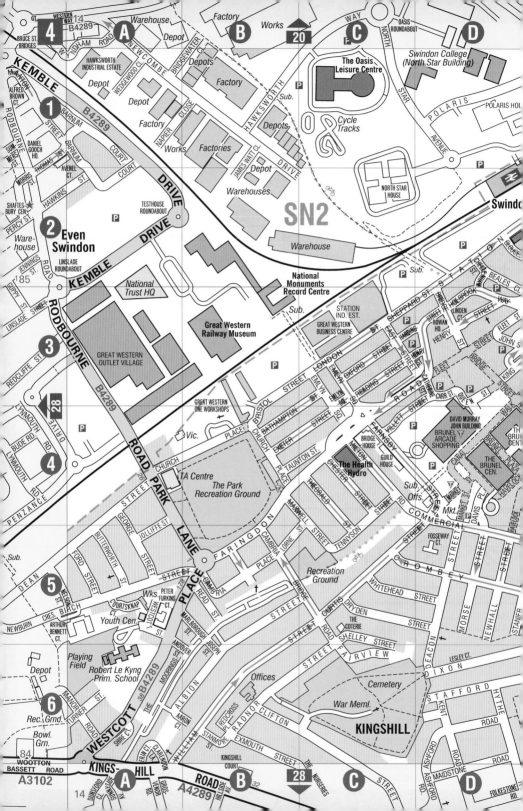

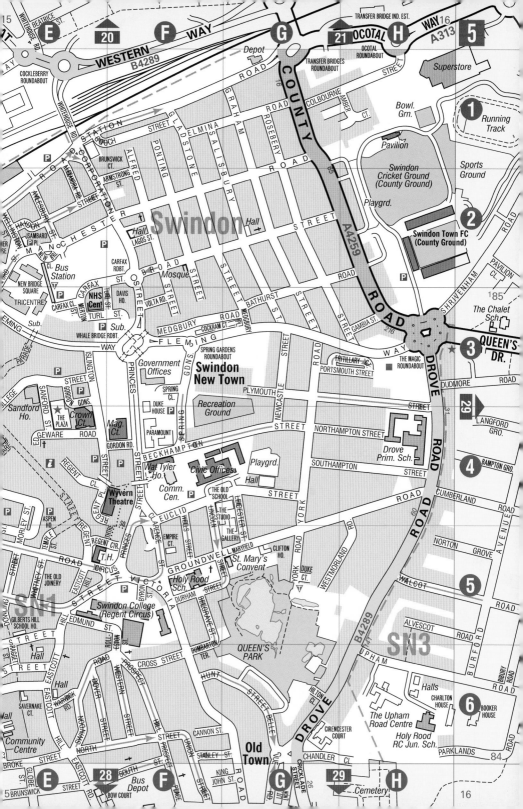

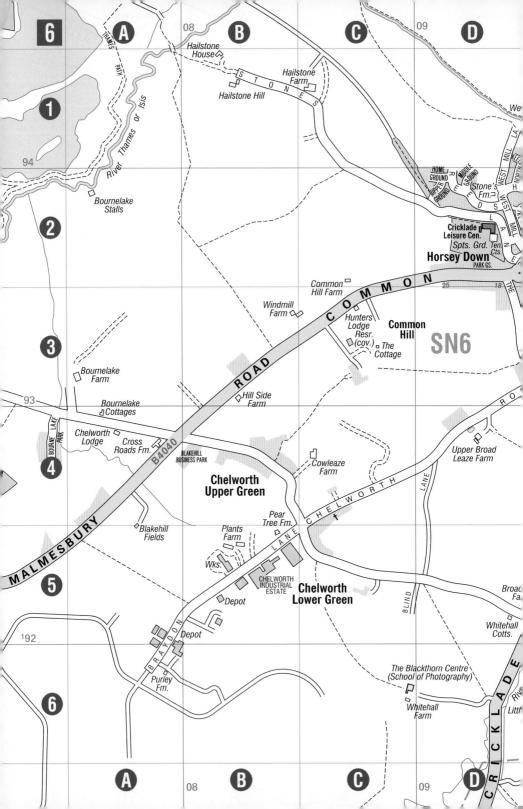

6

A · 08 · B · C · 09 · D

1

94

River Thames or Isis

Thames Path

Hailstone House

Hailstone Farm

S T O N E S

Hailstone Hill

Hailstone Hill

We

HOME
GROUND

MIDDLE
GROUND

UPPER
GROUND

Stone's
Fm.

WEST MILL LA.

WORTH

WEST MILL LANE

H

2

Bournelake
Stalls

Cricklade
Leisure Cen.

Spts. Grd. Ten.
Cts.

Horsey Down

PARK GS.

3

Bournelake
Farm

Common
Hill Farm

Windmill
Farm

Hunters
Lodge
Resr.
(cov.)

The
Cottage

**Common
Hill**

SN6

R O A D   C O M M O N

25 18

THE

RO

93

Bournelake
Cottages

BOURNE LANE PARK

Hill Side
Farm

4

Chelworth
Lodge

Cross
Roads Fm.

B4040

BLAKEHILL
BUSINESS PARK

Cowleaze
Farm

**Chelworth
Upper Green**

CHELWORTH

LANE

Upper Broad
Leaze Farm

5

Blakehill
Fields

Plants
Farm

Pear
Tree Fm.

Wks.

LANE

CHELWORTH INDUSTRIAL ESTATE

**Chelworth
Lower Green**

BLIND

Broad
Fa

M A L M E S B U R Y

Depot

192

Depot

BRAYDON

Whitehall
Cotts.

The Blackthorn Centre
(School of Photography)

6

Purley
Fm.

Whitehall
Farm

River
Littl

C R I C K L A D E

A · 08 · B · C · 09 · D

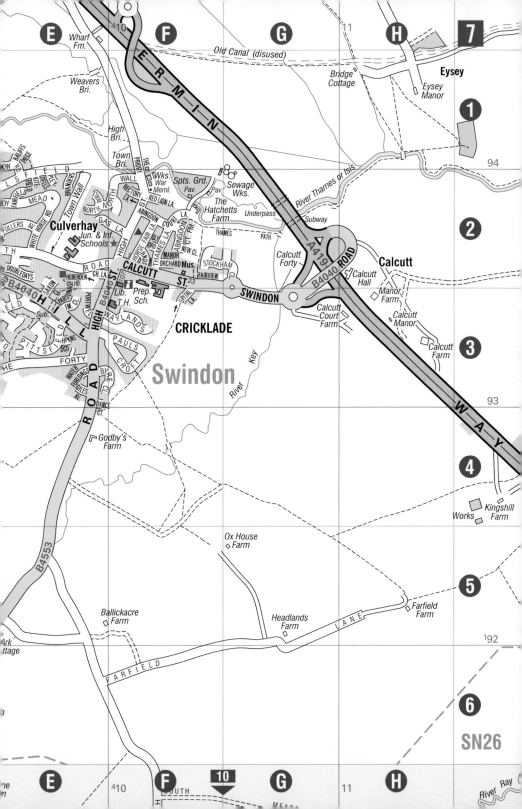

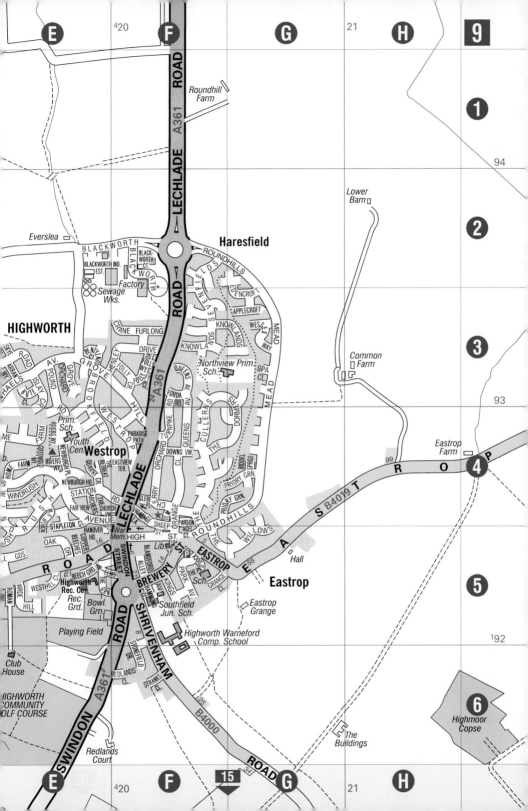

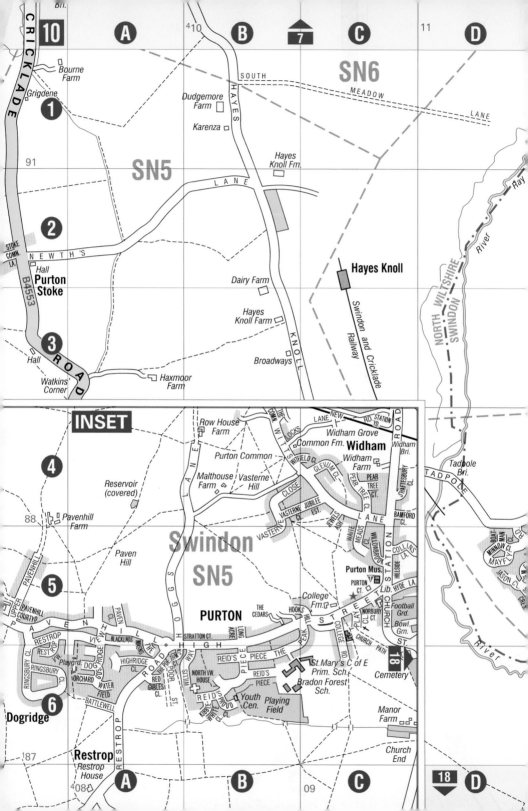

10

A 410 B 7 C 11 D

CRICKLADE

Bri.

Bourne Farm

SN6

Grigdene

1

SOUTH

HAYES

MEADOW

LANE

Dudgemore Farm

91

SN5

Karenza

LANE

Hayes Knoll Fm.

River Ray

NORTH WILTSHIRE

SWINDON

STOKE COMN. LA.

NEWTH'S

2

LANE

Hall

Purton Stoke

B4553

Dairy Farm

Hayes Knoll

KNOLL

Hayes Knoll

Swindon and Cricklade Railway

ROAD

3

Hall

Hayes Knoll Farm

Watkins' Corner

Broadways

Haxmoor Farm

INSET

Row House Farm

NEW

RD STATION YD

LANE

Widham Grove

COMN.

WITS.

ROAD

Common Fm.

Widham

Widham Bri.

LOCKS

Tadpole Bri.

TADPOLE

4

Reservoir (covered)

Purton Common

LANE

INTFIELD CL.

Widham Farm

PEAR TREE CT.

Widham

GLEVUM CL.

CHAFTESBURY CL.

Malthouse Farm

Vasterne Hill

CLOSE

PEAR TREE LA.

88

Pavenhill Farm

VASTERNE CL.

JUBILEE EST.

BAMFORD CL.

JEWELS

ASH

COLLOWBROOK

COLLINS LA.

HILLSIDE

River

BOAT MAN RD

MINNOW CL.

Swindon

SN5

Paven Hill

GIGGS

VASTERN

WHITE MEADS CL.

Purton Mus.

MAYFLY

JASON CL.

5

UPPER PAVENHILL

PAVENHILL COURTYD

HIGH

PURTON CT.

Lib.

HYDE LA.

College Fm.

PURTON

PAVEN CL.

BLACKLNDS

THE CEDARS

HOOKS

HILL

STREET

Football Grd.

Bowl. Grn.

RESTROP

VIEW RIDGE VW.

HIGHRIDGE CL.

ROAD

STRATTON CT.

ACRE

LONG

PEAK

COLLEGE RD.

NORBURY CT.

CHURCH

Playgrd.

DOG'S

RED GABLES CL.

SHE RW POO PUR ST.

WILLIS WAY

REID'S

PIECE

THE PIECE

CHURCH PATH

PLAYING GRN.

18

RINGSBURY CL.

RABISSONS CL.

REST

ORCHARD

WATER FIELD

NORTH VW. HOUSE

REID'S PIECE

St.Mary's C of E Prim. Sch.

Cemetery

6

BATTLEWELL

KIBBLE CL.

WYATT CL.

PROUD CL.

Youth Cen.

Playing Field

Bradon Forest Sch.

Dogridge

REID'S

Manor Farm

187

Restrop

RESTROP ROAD

Restrop House

Church End

408

A B 09 C **18** D

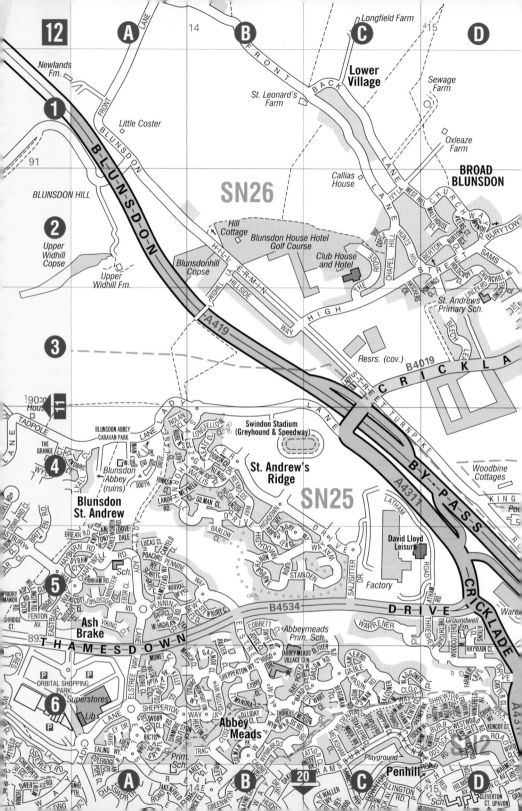

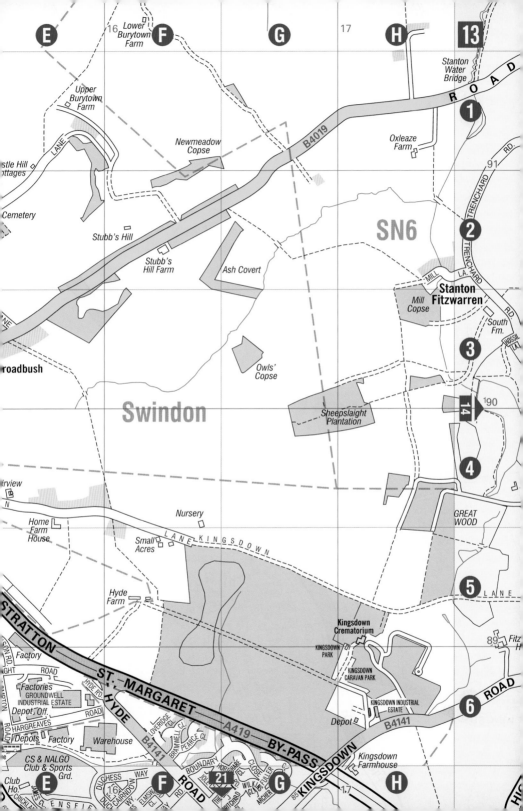

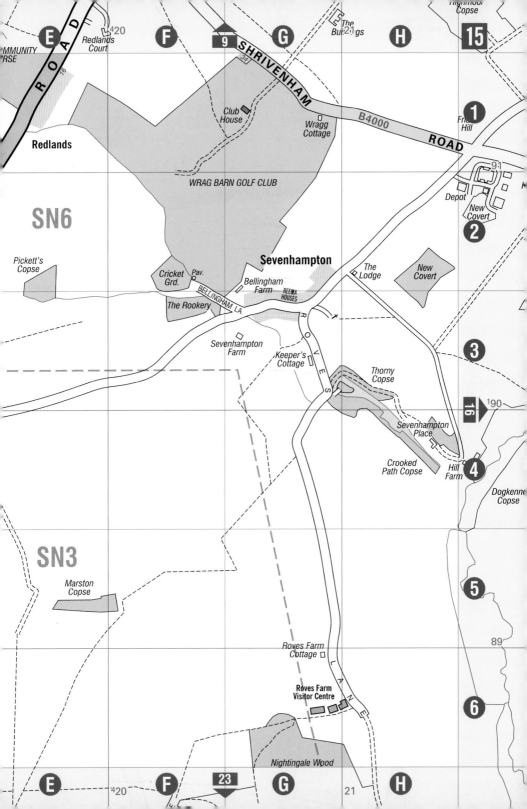

E **F** **9** SHRIVENHAM **G** The Buildings **H** **15**

420
Redlands
Court

COMMUNITY
HORSE

ROAD

B4000 ROAD

Fri...
Hill

1

Redlands

Club
House

Wragg
Cottage

91

Depot

New
Covert

2

SN6

WRAG BARN GOLF CLUB

Pickett's
Copse

Sevenhampton

Cricket
Grd.

Pav.

Bellingham
Farm

REEMA
HOUSES

The
Lodge

New
Covert

The Rookery

BELLINGHAM LA.

Sevenhampton
Farm

Keeper's
Cottage

R
O
V
E
S

Thorny
Copse

3

Sevenhampton
Place

16 190

Crooked
Path Copse

Hill
Farm

4

Dogkennel
Copse

SN3

Marston
Copse

5

89

Roves Farm
Cottage

L
A
N
E

Roves Farm
Visitor Centre

6

Nightingale Wood

E **F** **23** **G** **H**

420 21

16

Highmoor Copse

A 22 **B** **C** 23 **D**

Round Robin Farm

1 Friars Hill

SHRIVENHAM RD.

Folly Plantation

Round Robin Wood

VALE OF WHITE HORSE

SWINDON

B4000

B4508

Westmill Bri.

91

Depot

New Covert

Keeper's Lodge

Westmill Cotts.

2

New Covert

Coombes Copse

HIGHWORTH

Westmill Farm

Pennyhooks

Little Coombes Copse

Friarsmill Bridge

Friars Farm

Swan's Nest Copse

3

Cole

River

Homegrown Copse

Swindon

190 **15**

Sevenhampton Place

R O A D

PENNYHOOKS

PEN

Crooked th Copse

Hill Farm

4

SN6

B4000

HIGHWORTH

Dogkennel Copse

Sandhill Farm

Sandhill Farm Cotts.

Hurststone Barn

5 89

STALLPITS

LANE

STALLPITS

SAND

Stallpits Farm

FARLEIGH RD.

DAMSON

MOK CT.

A420

FORREST CL.

COLTON

CURTIS

6

FRIA RD

CLE COURT

COLTON

RBLO

Rhyme's House

SEND

Acorn Way

TOWN

A Lowerfield Wood 22 **B** **C** 23 Swanhill Farm **D**

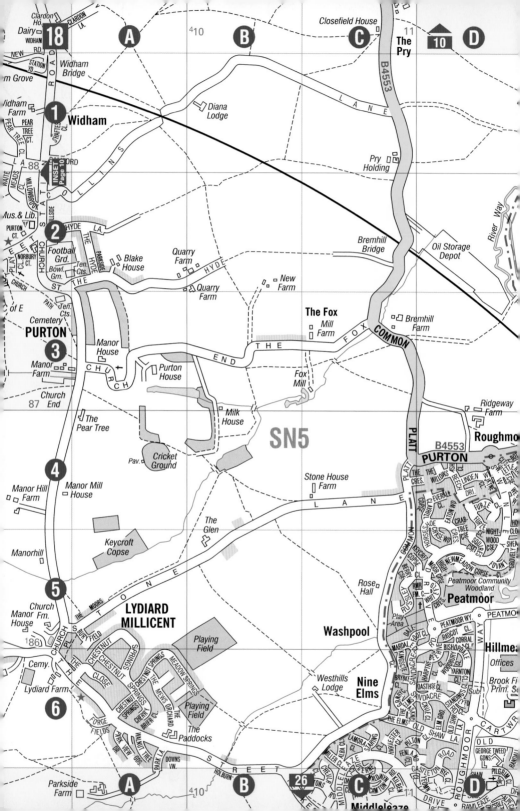

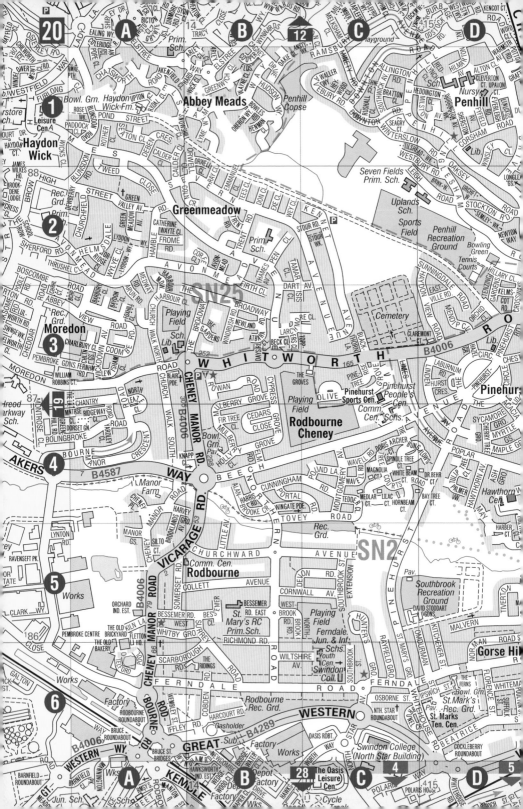

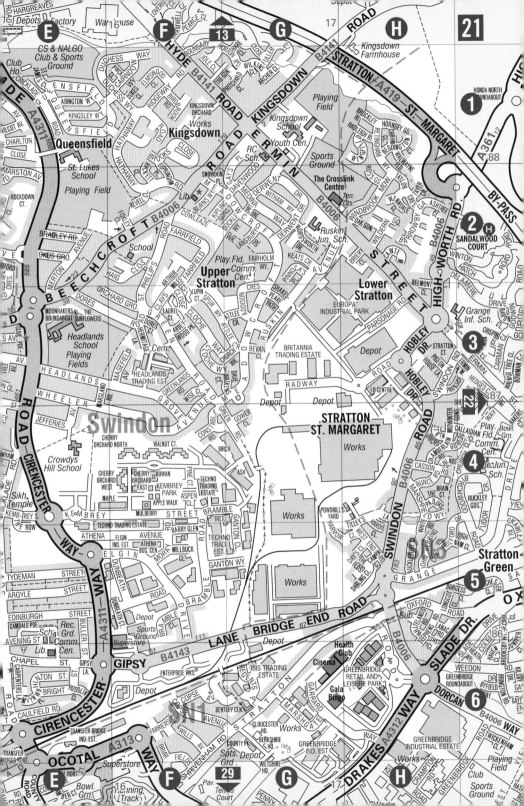

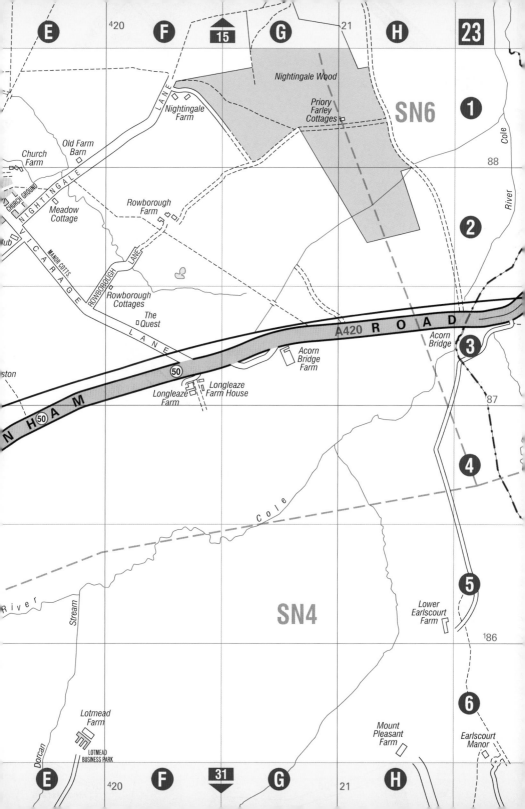

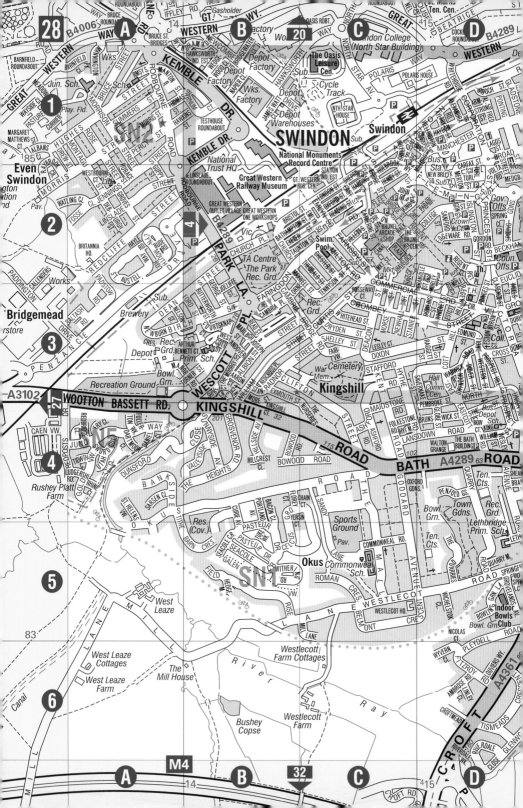

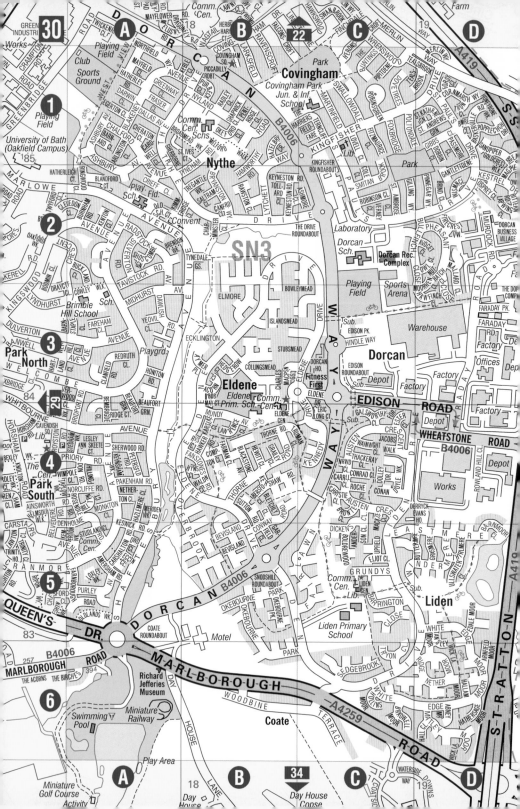

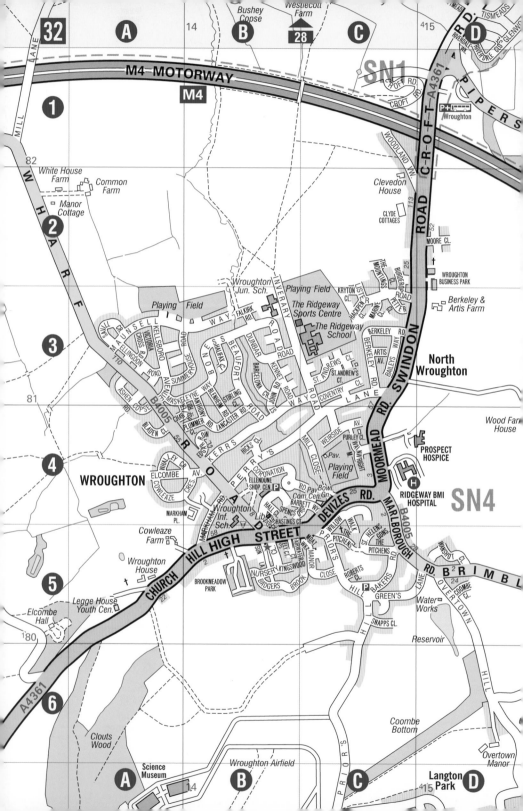

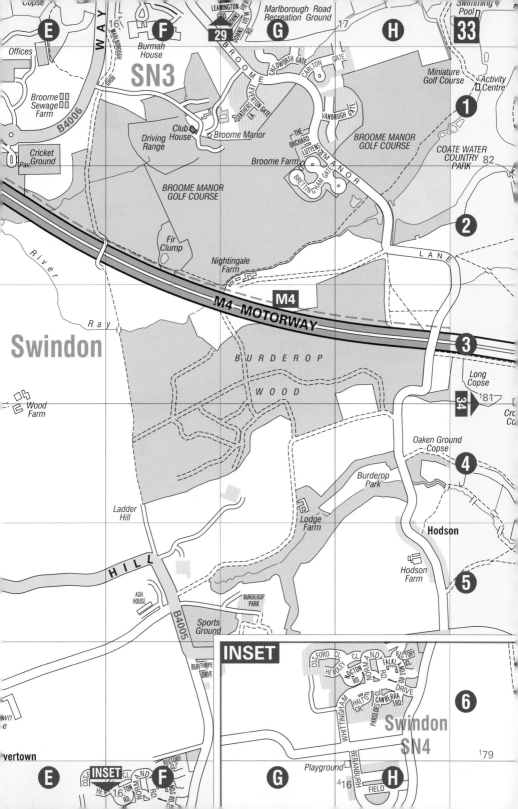

E · **F** · **29** · **G** · 17 · **H** · **33**

WAY · BROOME · ROAD

LEAMINGTON RD · DOWNS VIEW RD.

16 · MARLBOROUGH

Offices

Burmah House

SN3

Marlborough Road Recreation Ground

Swimming Pool

CALDWORTH GATE · CARLTON GATE

Miniature Golf Course

Activity Centre

1

Broome Sewage Farm

STAVERTON GATE LA.

Club House

Driving Range

Broome Manor

VANBRUGH GATE

Broome Farm

THE ORCHARD

LUTYENS

GM GATE

BRETTINGHAM GATE

BROOME MANOR GOLF COURSE

COATE WATER COUNTRY PARK 82

Cricket Ground

Pav.

0

B4006

BROOME MANOR GOLF COURSE

MANOR

2

Fir Clump

Nightingale Farm

LANE

River · Ray

M4 MOTORWAY · **M4**

3

Swindon

B U R D E R O P

W O O D

Long Copse

34 · 181

Cro Co

Wood Farm

Oaken Ground Copse

Burderop Park

4

Ladder Hill

Lodge Farm

Hodson

HILL

ASH HOUSE

BURDEROP PARK

Sports Ground

B4005

BURTHRPE DRIVE

Hodson Farm

5

INSET

COOSFORD CL · CL · RECTORY CL

HEADLEY · UCTON RD. · NORMANDY · FALKLANDS RD. · DRIVE

WHITTINGHAM · HALTON CR · PARSLOES · CANBERRA TRD.

Swindon

SN4

6

vertown

E · **INSET** · **F** · **G** · **H**

COO CL · HE · NORMANDY RD. · RECTORY CLF.

16 TON RD.

Playground

BERANBURH · FIELD

179

416

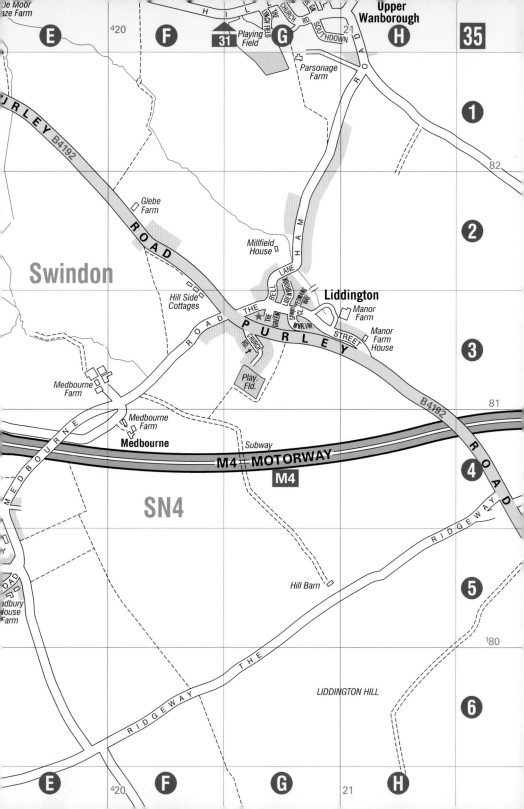

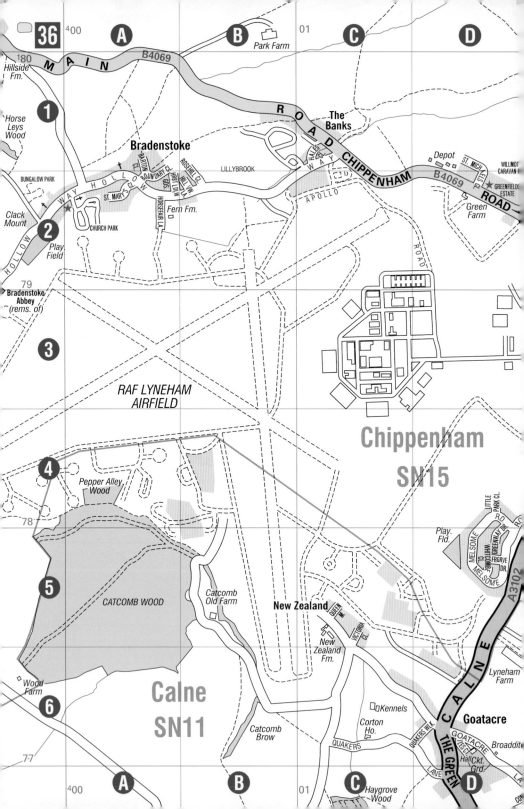

Including Streets, Places & Areas, Hospitals etc., Industrial Estates,
Selected Flats & Walkways, Stations and Selected Places of Interest.

HOW TO USE THIS INDEX

1. Each street name is followed by its Postcode District, then by its Locality abbreviation(s) and then by its map reference;
   e.g. **Abbey Vw. Rd.** SN25: Swin . . . .3H **19** is in the SN25 Postcode District and the Swindon Locality and is to be found in square 3H on page **19**.
   The page number is shown in bold type.

2. A strict alphabetical order is followed in which Av., Rd., St., etc. (though abbreviated) are read in full and as part of the street name;
   e.g. **Churchward Av.** appears after **Church Wlk. Sth.** but before **Church Way**

3. Streets and a selection of flats and walkways too small to be shown on the maps, appear in the index with the thoroughfare to which it is connected
   shown in brackets; e.g. **Baileys Farm Gdns.** SN3: Swin . . . .2H **29** (off Buckhurst Cres.)

4. Addresses that are in more than one part are referred to as not continuous.

5. Places and areas are shown in the index in BLUE TYPE and the map reference is to the actual map square in which the town centre or area is located
   and not to the place name shown on the map; e.g. BRADENSTOKE 2A 36

6. An example of a selected place of interest is Cricklade Mus. 2F 7

7. An example of a station is Swindon Station (Rail) . . . .2D 4 (1C 28). Included are Rail (Rail) and Park & Ride
   e.g. **Copse (Park & Ride)** 6E 13

8. An example of a Hospital, Walk-in Centre or Hospice is GREAT WESTERN HOSPITAL, THE 1C 34

9. Map references for entries that appear on large scale pages **4** & **5** are shown first, with small scale map references shown in brackets;
   e.g. **Albion St.** SN1: Swin 6B **4** (3B **28**)

GENERAL ABBREVIATIONS

All. : Alley	**Fld.** : Field	**Pk.** : Park
App. : Approach	**Flds.** : Fields	**Pl.** : Place
Arc. : Arcade	**Gdn.** : Garden	**Ri.** : Rise
Av. : Avenue	**Gdns.** : Gardens	**Rd.** : Road
Bri. : Bridge	**Ga.** : Gate	**Rdbt.** : Roundabout
Bldg. : Building	**Gt.** : Great	**Shop.** : Shopping
Bus. : Business	**Grn.** : Green	**Sth.** : South
Cvn. : Caravan	**Gro.** : Grove	**Sq.** : Square
Cen. : Centre	**Ho.** : House	**St.** : Street
Cir. : Circus	**Ind.** : Industrial	**Ter.** : Terrace
Cl. : Close	**Info.** : Information	**Trad.** : Trading
Comn. : Common	**La.** : Lane	**Up.** : Upper
Cotts. : Cottages	**Lit.** : Little	**Va.** : Vale
Ct. : Court	**Mnr.** : Manor	**Vw.** : View
Cres. : Crescent	**Mdw.** : Meadow	**Vis.** : Visitors
Cft. : Croft	**Mdws.** : Meadows	**Wlk.** : Walk
Dr. : Drive	**M.** : Mews	**W.** : West
E. : East	**Mus.** : Museum	**Yd.** : Yard
Ent. : Enterprise	**Nth.** : North	
Est. : Estate	**Pde.** : Parade	

LOCALITY ABBREVIATIONS

Ash K : **Ashton Keynes**	Hook : **Hook**	Shriv : **Shrivenham**
Bad : **Badbury**	Leigh : **Leigh**	S Mars : **South Marston**
Blun : **Blunsdon**	Lidd : **Liddington**	Stan F : **Stanton Fitzwarren**
Brad : **Bradenstoke**	Long : **Longcot**	Stra S : **Stratton St Margaret**
Burd : **Burderop**	Lyd M : **Lydiard Millicent**	Swin : **Swindon**
Calc : **Calcutt**	Lyd T : **Lydiard Tregoze**	Tock : **Tockenham**
Chi : **Chiseldon**	Lyne : **Lyneham**	Wan : **Wanborough**
Crick : **Cricklade**	New Z : **New Zealand**	Watch : **Watchfield**
Daun L : **Dauntsey Lock**	Pres : **Preston**	Wid : **Widham**
Goat : **Goatacre**	Pur : **Purton**	Woot B : **Wootton Bassett**
Hann : **Hannington**	Pur S : **Purton Stoke**	Wro : **Wroughton**
High : **Highworth**	Rest : **Restrop**	
Hod : **Hodson**	Seven : **Sevenhampton**	

I O Cen. SN3: Stra S 3H 21

A

ABBEY MEADS 6B 12
Abbey Meads Village Cen. SN25: Swin 6B 12
Abbey Rd. SN6: Watch 5H 17
Abbey Vw. Rd. SN25: Swin 3H 19
Abbeywood Pk. SN2: Stra S 3F 21
Abbotsbury Way SN25: Swin 5B 12
Abingdon Ct. Farm SN6: Crick 2F 7
Abingdon Ct. La. SN6: Crick 2F 7
Abington Way SN2: Stra S 1E 21
Abney Moor SN3: Swin 6D 30
Acacia Gro. SN2: Swin 4D 20
Acorn Cl. SN3: Swin 3B 30

Acorns, The SN3: Swin 6H 29
Addinsell Rd. SN25: Swin 4H 11
Addison Cres. SN2: Stra S 3G 21
Aden Ct. SN25: Swin 6A 12
Adwalton Cl. SN5: Swin 4E 27
Affleck Cl. SN5: Swin 3F 27
Aiken Rd. SN25: Swin 1F 19
Ainsworth Rd. SN3: Swin 4H 29
Akenfield Cl. SN25: Swin 1A 20
Akers Ct. SN26: Blun 2D 12
Akers Rdbt. SN2: Swin 3G 19
Akers Way SN2: Swin 3G 19
Alanbrooke Cres. SN5: Swin 4B 20
Alba Cl. SN5: Swin 6C 18
Albany Cl. SN3: Swin 3G 29
Albert St. SN1: Swin 4E 29
Albion St. SN1: Swin 6B 4 (3B 28)
Aldborough Cl. SN5: Swin 1F 27
Aldbourne Cl. SN2: Swin 6D 12
Alder Cl. SN2: Swin 2G 19

Alderley Rd. SN25: Swin 5H 11
Alderney Cl. SN4: Woot B 3F 25
Alexandra Rd. SN1: Swin 2E 5 (1D 28)
Alfred Brown Ct. SN2: Swin 1A 4
Alfred St. SN1: Swin 1F 5 (1D 28)
Alicia Cl. SN25: Swin 6F 11
Allington Rd. SN2: Swin 1C 20
Alnwick SN5: Swin 4E 27
Alpine Cl. SN5: Swin 1D 26
Alton Cl. SN2: Swin 1D 20
Alvescot Rd. SN3: Swin 5H 5 (3E 29)
Alveston Cl. SN3: Swin 2G 27
Alwyn Cl. SN5: Swin 5G 11
Amber Ct. SN1: Swin 1H 5 (1E 29)
Amberley Cl. SN25: Swin 2D 20
Ambrose Rd. SN1: Swin 6D 28
Amersham Rd. SN3: Swin 5A 30
Amesbury Cl. SN2: Swin 6D 12
Ancona Cl. SN5: Swin 1D 26
Anderson Cl. SN3: Swin 5C 30

Eliot Cl.—Goldcrest Wlk.

Eliot Cl. SN3: Swin 5C 30
Elizabeth Ho. SN3: Swin 2G 29
Ellendune Shop. Cen. SN4: Wro 4B 32
Ellingdon Rd. SN4: Wro 3A 32
Elm Cl. SN4: Woot B 1D 24
SN15: Lyne 3G 37
Elm Ct. SN4: Woot B 4C 24
Elm Gro. SN5: Swin 6D 18
Elmina Rd. SN1: Swin 1F 5 (1D 28)
Elmore SN3: Swin 3B 30
Elm Pk. SN4: Woot B 4C 24
Elm Rd. SN2: Swin 4B 20
Elms, The SN5: Swin 6C 18
SN6: High 5E 9
Elmswood Cl. SN2: Stra S 1F 21
Elsham Way SN25: Swin 1A 20
Elsie Hazel Ct. SN5: Swin 4D 26
Elstree Way SN25: Swin 6A 12
Ely Cl. SN5: Swin 4F 27
Ely Ct. SN4: Wro 5B 32
Embankment Rdbt. SN3: Swin 5E 29
Emerson Cl. SN25: Swin 6B 12
Emlyn Sq. SN1: Swin 3C 4 (2C 28)
Emmanuel Cl. SN25: Swin 2B 20
Empire Ct. SN1: Swin 5F 5
Endeavour Rd. SN3: Stra S 6A 22
Enford Av. SN2: Swin 6D 12
Englefield SN4: Woot B 4D 24
Ensor Cl. SN25: Swin 4B 12
Enterprise Works SN2: Swin 6F 21
Eric Long Ct. SN3: Swin 4C 30
Erin Ct. SN1: Swin 6A 4 (3B 28)
Erlestoke Way SN2: Swin 6D 12
Ermin M. SN3: Stra S 3A 22
Ermin St. SN2: Stra S 1G 21
SN3: Stra S 3A 22
SN26: Blun 2B 12
Ermin Way SN6: Calc, Crick 1F 7
Eshton Wlk. SN3: Swin 5H 29
Espringham Ho. *SN2: Stra S* *2F 21*
(off Hathaway Rd.)
Espringham Pl. SN2: Stra S 2F 21
Essex Wlk. SN3: Swin 2G 29
Estella Cl. SN25: Swin 6G 11
Euclid St. SN1: Swin 4F 5 (2D 28)
Europa Ind. Pk. SN3: Stra S 3G 21
Europark SN5: Swin 6C 26
Euroway SN5: Swin 6C 26
Eveleigh Rd. SN4: Woot B 3D 24
Evelyn St. SN3: Swin 5E 29
EVEN SWINDON 2A 4 (1H 27)
Evergreens Cl. SN3: Stra S 5B 22
Everleigh Rd. SN2: Swin 1D 20
Eworth Cl. SN5: Swin 3C 26
Exbury Cl. SN25: Swin 6B 12
Exe Cl. SN25: Swin 2B 20
Exeter St. SN1: Swin 4B 4 (2B 28)
Exmoor Cl. SN25: Swin 2F 19
Exmouth St. SN1: Swin 6B 4 (3B 28)
Eyre Cl. SN25: Swin 6F 11
EYSEY 1H 7

F

Fairfax Cl. SN3: Swin 1G 29
Fairfield SN4: Woot B 2D 24
SN6: Crick 2E 7
Fairford Cres. SN25: Swin 2E 21
Fairholm Way SN2: Stra S 2G 21
Fairlawn SN3: Swin 5C 30
Fairleigh Cres. SN3: Swin 5F 29
Fairthorne Way SN6: Shriv 6E 17
Fair Vw. SN6: High 4E 9
Fairview SN1: Swin 6C 4 (3C 28)
SN6: Crick 2F 7
Fairwater Ct. SN4: Wro 5B 32
Falconer M. SN25: Swin 6C 12
Falconscroft SN3: Swin 6B 22
Falkirk Rd. SN4: Wro 3B 32
Falklands Rd. SN4: Wro 6H 33
Falmouth Gro. SN3: Swin 4F 29
Fanstones Rd. SN3: Swin 4B 30
Faraday Pk. SN3: Swin 3D 30
Faraday Rd. SN3: Swin 4D 30
Fareham Cl. SN3: Swin 3A 30
Farfield La. SN6: Crick 6F 7
Faringdon Rd. SN1: Swin 5B 4 (3B 28)
SN6: Shriv 5F 17
SN6: Watch 4G 17
Farleigh Rd. SN6: Shriv 6D 16
Farman Cl. SN3: Swin 4B 30
Farmer Cres. SN25: Swin 6D 12
Farmhouse La. SN1: Swin 1F 29
Farnborough Rd. SN3: Swin 5A 30
Farne Way SN4: Woot B 3F 25
Farnsby St. SN1: Swin 4C 4 (2C 28)
Farrfield SN2: Stra S 2F 21
Farriers Cl. SN1: Swin 6F 21
Farthing La. SN15: Lyne 1E 37
Fawley Cl. SN25: Swin 4F 11
Feather Wood SN5: Swin 3G 27
Fenby Pl. SN25: Swin 5G 11
Fenland Cl. SN5: Swin 6C 18
Fennel Cl. SN2: Swin 2G 19
Fenton Av. SN25: Swin 5H 11
Ferndale Rd. SN2: Swin 6A 20
Fernham Rd. SN25: Swin 3A 20
Ferns, The SN2: Swin 6D 20
Ferrers Dr. SN5: Swin 4C 26
Fessey Ho. SN25: Swin 1H 19
Fiddle, The SN6: Crick 3D 6
Fieldfare SN3: Swin 1C 30
Field Ri. SN1: Swin 5B 28
Fields, The SN3: Stra S 5H 21
Figsbury Cl. SN25: Swin 1F 19
Filsham Rd. SN25: Swin 5F 11
Finchdale SN3: Swin 6C 22
Firecrest Vw. SN3: Swin 2D 30
Firethorn Cl. SN2: Swin 5D 20
Firth Cl. SN25: Swin 3B 20
Fir Tree Cl. SN2: Swin 4B 20
Fitkin Ct. SN25: Swin 5G 11
Fitness First Health Club
Swindon Central 3C 30
Swindon West 1F 27
Fitwell Rd. SN25: Swin 5F 11
Fitzmaurice Cl. SN3: Swin 1C 30
Fitzpiers Cl. SN25: Swin 1F 19
Fitzroy Rd. SN1: Swin 6D 28
Fiveways Rdbt. SN5: Swin 2E 27
Fleet St. SN1: Swin 3D 4 (2C 28)
Fleetwood Ct. SN5: Swin 5D 26
Fleming Way SN1: Swin 3E 5 (2D 28)
Fletton Ho. SN2: Swin 5A 20
Flint Hill SN5: Swin 4F 27
Florence St. SN2: Swin 6D 20
Florey Ct. SN1: Swin 4B 28
Folkestone Rd. SN1: Swin 6D 4 (4C 28)
Folly Cl. SN6: High 3F 9
Folly Cres. SN6: High 3F 9
SN6: Watch 3G 17
Folly Dr. SN6: High 3F 9
Folly Way SN6: High 3F 9
Fonthill Wlk. SN3: Swin 3F 29
Ford St. SN1: Swin 5A 4 (3B 28)
Forester Cl. SN3: Swin 4C 30
Forge Flds. SN5: Lyd M 6A 18
Forrest Cl. SN6: Shriv 6D 16
Forsey Cl. SN3: Swin 1D 30
Forty, The SN6: Crick 3E 7
Forum, The SN5: Swin 3F 27
Forum Cl. SN3: Stra S 6B 22
Fosse Cl. SN2: Swin 2A 28
Fosseway Ct. SN1: Swin 5D 4 (3C 28)
Foundry Ri. SN4: Chi 6C 34
Fovant Cl. SN5: Swin 5D 18
Fowey SN5: Swin 5D 26
FOX, THE 3C 18
Fox, The SN5: Pur 3B 18
Foxbridge SN3: Swin 1C 30
Fox Brook SN4: Woot B 3E 25
Foxglove Rd. SN25: Swin 1G 19
Foxhill Cl. SN25: Swin 3A 20
Foxleaze SN6: Crick 1E 7
Foxley Cl. SN2: Stra S 2F 21
Fox Wood SN5: Swin 3G 27
Frampton Cl. SN5: Swin 2E 27
Francomes SN25: Swin 2H 19
Frankel Av. SN25: Swin 5G 11
Frankland Rd. SN5: Swin 5B 26
Franklin Ho. *SN3: Swin* *6A 22*
(off Twickenham Cl.)
Frankton Gdns. SN3: Stra S 4A 22
Frank Warman Ct. SN3: Stra S 3A 22
Fraser Cl. SN3: Swin 1A 30
Freegrove Dr. SN15: Lyne 5D 36
FRESHBROOK 4D 26
Freshbrook Cen. SN5: Swin 5D 26
Freshbrook Rdbt. SN5: Swin 4D 26
Freshbrook Way SN5: Swin 4E 27
Friars Cl. SN6: Shriv 6D 16
Friday St. SN25: Swin 6F 11
Friesian Cl. SN5: Swin 1D 26
Friesland Cl. SN5: Swin 1D 26
Frilford Dr. SN3: Stra S 5H 21
Frith Copse SN5: Swin 4D 18
Fritillary Ct. SN1: Swin 3H 5
Frobisher Dr. SN3: Swin 2G 29
Frome Rd. SN25: Swin 2A 20
Front La. SN26: Blun 1A 12
Fry Cl. SN5: Swin 4A 28
Fuller Cl. SN2: Stra S 1G 21
Fuller Gdns. SN3: S Mars 2D 22
Fullers Av. SN6: Crick 2E 7
Fullerton Wlk. SN5: Swin 4A 28
Furlong Cl. SN25: Swin 1H 19
Furze Cl. SN5: Swin 4D 18
Fyfield Av. SN2: Swin 1D 20
Fyne Cl. SN5: Swin 4E 19

G

Gable Cl. SN25: Swin 6C 12
Gablecross Rdbt. SN3: S Mars 4D 22
Gabriel Cres. SN25: Swin 4F 11
Gainsborough Av. SN4: Woot B 2D 24
Gainsborough Ct. SN5: Swin 3D 26
Gainsborough Way SN5: Swin 3D 26
Gairlock Cl. SN5: Swin 4E 19
Gala Bingo
Swindon 6G 21
Galen Vw. SN1: Swin 5B 28
Gallery, The SN1: Swin 5G 5
Galley Orchard SN6: Crick 2F 7
Galloway Cl. SN5: Swin 1D 26
Galloway Rd. SN25: Swin 1F 19
Galsworthy Cl. SN3: Swin 4C 30
Galton Way SN2: Swin 6H 19
Gambia St. SN1: Swin 3H 5 (2E 29)
Gamekeepers Cl. SN25: Swin 5A 12
Gantlettdene SN3: Swin 2D 30
Ganton Cl. SN2: Swin 5G 21
Ganton Way SN2: Swin 5F 21
Garden, The SN2: Stra S 1F 21
Gardens, The SN25: Swin 3B 20
Garfield Cl. SN3: Swin 5B 30
Garrard Way SN3: Swin 6G 21
Garraways SN4: Woot B 3F 25
Garsington Dr. SN25: Swin 6F 11
Garson Rd. SN25: Swin 6C 12
Gartons Rd. SN5: Swin 1C 26
Gas La. SN6: Crick 2F 7
Gaveller Rd. SN25: Swin 5F 11
Gaynor Cl. SN25: Swin 6B 12
Gay's Pl. SN2: Stra S 2G 21
Gayton Way SN3: Stra S 6A 22
George Gay Gdns. *SN3: Swin* *4G 29*
(off Kelham Cl.)
George Selman Gdns.
SN3: Swin *2H 29*
(off Twyford Cl.)
George St. SN1: Swin 4A 4 (3B 28)
George Tweed Gdns. SN5: Swin 6D 18
Gerard Wlk. SN5: Swin 2D 26
Gibbs Cl. SN3: Swin 1D 30
Gifford Rd. SN3: Stra S 3A 22
Gilberts Hill School Ho.
SN1: Swin 5E 5
Giles Av. SN6: Crick 3E 7
Giles Rd. SN25: Swin 6G 11
Gilling Way SN3: Swin 2C 30
Gilman Cl. SN25: Swin 4B 12
Giotto Cl. SN25: Swin 5E 11
Gipsy La. SN2: Swin 6E 21
Gladstone St. SN1: Swin 1F 5 (1D 28)
Gladys Plumley Gdns. *SN2: Swin* *6E 21*
(off Carpenters La.)
Glebe Pl. SN6: High 4F 9
Glebe Rd. SN4: Woot B 4C 24
Glenmore Cen., The SN5: Swin 6F 19
Glenmore Rd. SN25: Swin 1F 19
Glenville Cl. SN4: Woot B 5D 24
Glenwood Cl. SN1: Swin 6D 28
Glevum Cl. SN5: Pur 4C 10
Glevum Rd. SN3: Stra S 5B 22
Globe St. SN1: Swin 6E 5 (4D 28)
Gloucester Ho. SN1: Swin 6G 21
Gloucester St. SN1: Swin 2D 4 (1C 28)
GOATACRE 6D 36
Goatacre La. SN11: Goat 6D 36
Goddard Av. SN1: Swin 4C 28
Goddard Ct. *SN1: Swin* *4E 29*
(off Cricklade St.)
Godolphin Cl. SN5: Swin 5C 26
Godwin Ct. SN1: Swin 4E 29
Godwin Rd. SN3: Stra S 3A 22
Goldcrest Wlk. SN3: Swin 1D 30

A-Z Swindon 43

Goldsborough Cl.—Highworth Recreation Cen.

Goldsborough Cl. SN5: Swin 2E 27
Gold Vw. SN5: Swin 4A 28
Gooch St. SN1: Swin 1E 5 (1D 28)
Goodrich Ct. *SN5: Swin 4F 27*
(off Affleck Cl.)
Gordon Gdns. SN1: Swin 3E 5 (2D 28)
Gordon Rd. SN1: Swin 4F 5 (2D 28)
Gore Cl. SN25: Swin 6A 12
GORSE HILL 6E 21
Gosling Cl. SN4: Wan 5G 31
Goughs Way SN4: Woot B 3E 25
Goulding Cl. SN3: Stra S 4H 21
Gower Cl. SN2: Stra S 4G 21
SN5: Swin 3C 26
Grace Wlk. SN25: Swin 6G 11
Grafton Rd. SN2: Swin 1D 20
Graham St. SN1: Swin 1G 5 (1E 29)
Grailey Cl. SN3: Swin 4B 30
Granary Cl. SN5: Swin 6C 18
Grandison Cl. SN5: Swin 2D 26
Grange, The SN25: Blun 4H 11
Grange Cl. SN4: Wan 5G 31
SN6: High 5F 9
Grange Dr. SN3: Stra S 5H 21
GRANGE PARK 4C 26
Grange Pk. *SN5: Swin 3D 26*
(off Grange Pk. Way)
Grange Pk. Way SN5: Swin 3C 26
Granica Cl. SN25: Swin 6G 11
Grantham Cl. SN5: Swin 5E 27
Grantley Cl. SN3: Swin 5H 29
Granville St. SN1: Swin 5E 5 (2D 28)
Grasmere SN3: Swin 5D 30
Graythwaite Cl. SN25: Swin 6A 12
Gt. Western Bus. Cen.
SN1: Swin 3C 4 (2C 28)
GREAT WESTERN HOSPITAL, THE 1C 34
Gt. Western One Workshops
SN1: Swin 3B 4 (2B 28)
Gt. Western Outlet Village
SN2: Swin 3A 4 (2B 28)
Great Western Railway Mus. 3B 4 (2B 28)
Gt. Western Way
SN2: Swin 1A 4 & 1E 5 (6B 20)
SN5: Swin 5B 26
Green, The SN4: Lidd 3G 35
SN4: Woot B 3F 25
SN6: High 5E 9
SN6: Shriv 6E 17
SN11: Goat 6D 36
SN15: Lyne 2E 37
Greenaway SN4: Wan 6G 31
Greenbridge Ind. Est. SN3: Swin 6G 21
(not continuous)
Greenbridge Retail and Leisure Pk.
SN3: Swin 6H 21
Greenbridge Rd. SN3: Swin 1H 29
Greenbridge Rdbt. SN3: Stra S 6H 21
Greenfields SN3: S Mars 1D 22
Greenfields Est. SN15: Lyne 2D 36
Greenham Wlk. *SN3: Swin 2H 29*
(off Marlowe Av.)
Greenhill Rd. SN2: Swin 4H 19
Greenlands Rd. SN2: Stra S 3F 21
Green La. SN4: Wan 4F 31
GREENMEADOW 2A 20
Green Mdw. Av. SN25: Swin 2A 20
Green Rd. SN2: Stra S 3F 21
Greensand Cl. SN25: Swin 5A 12
Green's La. SN4: Wro 5C 32
Green Valley Av. SN25: Swin 2A 20
Greenway SN4: Tock 1G 37
Greenway Cl. SN3: Swin 1A 30
Greenway Dr. SN15: Lyne 5D 36
Greenwich Cl. SN25: Swin 1B 20
Gresham Cl. SN3: Swin 2G 29
Greywethers Av. SN3: Swin 5F 29
Griffiths Cl. SN3: Stra S 5A 22
Grindal Dr. SN5: Swin 3C 26
Grosmont Dr. SN5: Swin 3E 27
Grosvenor Rd. SN1: Swin 6A 4 (4B 28)
Groundwell Ind. Est.
SN25: Swin 6E 13
Groundwell Rd. SN1: Swin 5F 5 (3D 28)
Grove Hill SN6: High 3E 9
Grovelands Av. SN1: Swin 5D 28
Grovely Cl. SN5: Swin 5D 18
Grove Orchard SN6: High 3E 9
Groves, The SN2: Swin 3B 20
Groves St. SN2: Swin 2A 28
Grundys SN3: Swin 5C 30
Guernsey La. SN25: Swin 6G 11
Guildford Av. SN3: Swin 5G 29
Guild Ho. SN1: Swin 4C 4
Guppy St. SN2: Swin 3A 4 (2A 28)

H

Hackett Cl. SN2: Stra S 2F 21
Hackleton Ri. SN3: Stra S 6A 22
Hackpen Cl. SN4: Wro 3C 32
Haddon Cl. SN5: Swin 3C 26
Hadleigh Cl. SN5: Swin 2F 27
Hadleigh Ri. SN3: Stra S 1H 21
Hadrians Cl. SN3: Stra S 6B 22
Haig Cl. SN2: Stra S 2F 21
Hales Cl. SN15: Lyne 1C 36
Halifax Cl. SN4: Wro 3B 32
Hallam Moor SN3: Swin 6D 30
Hall Cl. SN4: Wro 4B 32
Hallsfield SN6: Crick 2D 6
Halton Cres. SN4: Wro 6H 33
Hamble Rd. SN25: Swin 2A 20
Hamilton Cl. SN3: Swin 1G 29
Hammond Cl. SN6: High 5F 9
Hammonds SN6: Crick 2F 7
Hampshire Cl. SN5: Swin 1D 26
HAMPTON 5C 8
Hampton Dr. SN5: Swin 2C 26
Ham Rd. SN4: Lidd, Wan 6H 31
Hamstead Way SN25: Swin 5A 12
Hamworthy Rd. SN3: Swin 2B 30
Hanbury Rd. SN3: Swin 4G 29
Handel St. SN2: Swin 6D 20
HANNINGTON 3A 8
Hannington Cl. SN2: Swin 6C 12
Hanover Ct. *SN3: Swin 1C 30*
(off Kingfisher Dr.)
Hanover Ho. SN6: High 5E 9
Hanson Cl. SN5: Swin 6E 19
Harber Ct. SN2: Swin 5D 20
Harbour Cl. SN25: Swin 3A 20
Harbour Mdw. SN25: Swin 2A 20
Harcourt Rd. SN2: Swin 6B 20
Hardie Cl. SN3: Stra S 5H 21
Harding St. SN1: Swin 3C 4 (2C 28)
Hardwich Ho. *SN1: Swin 4D 28*
(off Prospect Pl.)
Hardwick Cl. SN25: Swin 1B 20
Hardy Cl. SN25: Swin 6G 11
Harebell Cl. SN25: Swin 1G 19
Hare Cl. SN2: Stra S 6G 13
HARESFIELD 2F 9
Hargreaves Rd. SN25: Swin 6E 13
Harlech Cl. SN5: Swin 4F 27
Harlestone Rd. SN3: Stra S 6A 22
Harold Thorpe Gdns. *SN3: Swin 2G 29*
(off Middleton Cl.)
Harptree Cl. SN5: Swin 6D 18
Harriers, The SN3: Swin 1C 30
Harrington Wlk. SN3: Swin 1G 29
Harris Rd. SN2: Swin 4B 20
Harrow Cl. SN3: Stra S 5G 21
Harrow Gro. SN15: Lyne 3F 37
Hart Cl. SN4: Woot B 5D 24
Hartington Rd. SN25: Swin 5F 11
Hartland Cl. SN3: Swin 3H 29
HARTS CLOSE 6E 37
Hartsthorn Cl. SN2: Swin 2G 19
Harvester Cl. SN5: Swin 6C 18
Harvey Gro. SN2: Swin 4A 20
Hastings Ct. SN4: Wro 4B 32
Hastings Dr. SN15: Lyne 3F 37
Hatchers Cres. SN26: Blun 2C 12
Hatch Rd. SN3: Stra S 2A 22
Hatfield Cl. SN25: Swin 6H 11
Hathaway Rd. SN2: Stra S 1F 21
Hatherall Cl. SN3: Stra S 4B 22
Hatherleigh Ct. SN3: Swin 2H 29
Hatherley Rd. SN3: Swin 1A 30
Hathersage Moor SN3: Swin 6D 30
Hatton Gro. SN3: Swin 2G 29
Havelock Sq. SN1: Swin 4D 4 (2C 28)
Havelock St. SN1: Swin 4D 4 (2C 28)
Haven Cl. SN3: Stra S 6A 22
Havisham Dr. SN25: Swin 6F 11
(not continuous)
Hawfinch Cl. SN3: Swin 3D 30
Hawker Rd. SN3: Swin 4B 30
Hawkins St. SN2: Swin 2A 4 (1A 28)
Hawkswood SN3: Swin 6C 22
Hawksworth Ind. Est. SN2: Swin 1A 4 (1B 28)
Hawksworth Way SN2: Swin 1B 4 (1B 28)
Hawthorn Av. SN2: Swin 4D 20
Hayburn Rd. SN25: Swin 5H 11
HAYDON 6H 11
Haydon Ct. SN25: Swin 1H 19
Haydon Ct. Dr. SN25: Swin 1H 19
Haydon End La. SN25: Swin 6F 11
Haydonleigh Dr. SN25: Swin 1H 19
Haydon St. SN1: Swin 2E 5 (1D 28)
Haydon Vw. Rd. SN25: Swin 2D 20
HAYDON WICK 2H 19
Haydon Wick Community Leisure Cen. 1H 19
Hayes Knoll SN5: Pur S 1B 10
Hayes Knoll Station
Swindon and Cricklade Railway 2C 10
(Tadpole La.)
Hay La. SN4: Woot B, Wro 6B 26
SN5: Swin 1C 26
(not continuous)
Hay La. Cvn. Pk. SN4: Wro 6D 26
Hayle Rd. SN2: Swin 2A 28
Haynes Cl. SN3: Swin 4B 30
Haywain Cl. SN25: Swin 6D 12
Hayward Cl. SN25: Swin 6B 12
Hazelbury Cres. SN3: Swin 1B 30
Hazel End SN4: Woot B 4D 24
Hazel Gro. SN2: Swin 3D 20
Hazells La. SN6: Shriv 6F 17
Hazlemere Cl. SN3: Swin 4A 30
Headlands Gro. SN2: Swin 3E 21
Headlands Trad. Est. SN2: Swin 3F 21
Headley Cl. SN4: Wro 6G 33
Health Hydro, The 4C 4 (2C 28)
Heathcote Cl. SN5: Swin 6E 19
Heath Way SN3: Stra S 6A 22
Heaton Cl. SN25: Swin 6B 12
Hebden Cl. SN25: Swin 5H 11
Heberden Ho. SN6: Crick 2E 7
Hector Rd. *SN25: Swin 5F 11*
(off Hartington Rd.)
Heddington Cl. SN2: Swin 1D 20
Hedgerow Cl. SN3: Swin 3B 30
Hedges, The SN4: Wan 5G 31
Hedges Cl. SN3: Stra S 3A 22
Heights, The SN1: Swin 4B 28
Helena Rd. SN25: Swin 4F 11
Helmsdale SN25: Swin 2A 20
Helmsdale Wlk. SN3: Swin 4H 29
Helston Rd. SN3: Swin 3H 29
Henchard Cres. SN25: Swin 1F 19
Henley Dr. SN6: High 3F 9
Henley Rd. SN3: Swin 4G 29
Henman Cl. SN25: Swin 1B 20
Henrietta Ct. *SN3: Swin 4E 29*
(off Marlborough Rd.)
Henry St. SN1: Swin 3D 4 (2C 28)
Hepworth Rd. SN25: Swin 6A 12
Herbert Harvey Ct. SN3: Stra S 6B 22
Herbert Ludlow Gdns. SN15: Brad 2A 36
Hereford Lawns SN3: Swin 5G 29
Hermitage, The SN3: Swin 4E 29
Hermitage La. SN2: Stra S 3F 21
Heronbridge Cl. SN5: Swin 3F 27
Heronscroft SN3: Swin 1C 30
Herschel Cl. SN25: Swin 5E 11
Hertford Cl. SN3: Swin 2G 29
Hesketh Cres. SN3: Swin 5E 29
Hewitt Cl. SN3: Swin 4B 30
Hexham Cl. SN5: Swin 3E 27
Heytsbury Gdns. SN5: Swin 4C 26
Heywood Cl. SN2: Swin 1C 20
Hicks Cl. SN4: Wro 4B 32
Hidcot Ct. SN25: Swin 5H 11
Highclere Av. SN3: Swin 4G 29
Highdown Way SN25: Swin 4B 12
Highfold SN4: Woot B 4E 25
Highland Cl. SN5: Swin 1D 26
High Mead SN4: Woot B 3E 25
Highmoor Copse SN5: Swin 5D 18
Highnam Cl. SN3: Stra S 5A 22
Highridge Cl. SN5: Pur 6A 10
High St. SN1: Swin 4E 29
SN4: Chi 6C 34
SN4: Wan 4H 31
SN4: Woot B 4C 24
SN4: Wro 5B 32
SN5: Pur 5B 10
SN6: Crick 3E 7
SN6: High 5F 9
SN6: Shriv 6E 17
SN6: Watch 2F 17
SN25: Swin 2H 19
SN26: Blun 3C 12
Highwood Cl. SN2: Swin 2G 19
HIGHWORTH 4F 9
Highworth Recreation Cen. 5E 9

44 A-Z Swindon

Lady La. SN25: Blun, Swin 5A 12
SN25: Swin 6A 12
SN26: Blun 3C 12
Lady Mead SN6: Crick 2E 7
Lagos St. SN1: Swin 2F 5 (1D 28)
Lake Rd. SN6: Shriv 5F 17
Lakeside SN3: Swin 5F 29
Lambert Cl. SN5: Swin 5E 27
Lambourn Av. SN3: Swin 5F 29
Lamora Cl. SN6: Swin 6C 18
Lampeter Rd. SN25: Swin 6F 11
Lanac Rd. SN3: Stra S 5H 21
Lancaster M. SN3: S Mars 6B 14
Lancaster Pl. SN3: S Mars 6B 14
Lancaster Rd. SN4: Wro 4B 32
Lancaster Sq. SN15: Lyne 3E 37
Landor Rd. SN25: Swin 4A 12
Lane, The SN2: Swin 3A 20
Langdale Dr. SN5: Swin 5E 27
Langford Gro. SN3: Swin 4H 5 (2F 29)
Langley Rd. SN5: Swin 5E 19
Langport Cl. SN5: Swin 4E 27
Langstone Way SN5: Swin 2F 27
LANGTON PARK 6D 32
Lanhydrock Cl. SN5: Swin 4D 26
Lansbury Dr. SN3: Stra S 2G 21
Lansdowne Ho. SN3: Swin 6A 22
(off Twickenham Cl.)
Lansdown Rd. SN1: Swin 4C 28
Lapwing Cl. SN3: Swin 2D 30
Larchmore Cl. SN25: Swin 3B 20
Larksfield SN3: Swin 1B 30
Latham Rd. SN25: Swin 4C 12
Latton Cl. SN2: Swin 6C 12
Laughton Way SN5: Swin 6B 12
Laurel Ct. SN2: Stra S 3F 21
Lavinia Wlk. SN25: Swin 6F 11
LAWN 5G 29
Lawns, The SN4: Woot B 3C 24
Lawrence Cl. SN3: Swin 4B 30
Lawton Cl. SN3: Swin 5H 29
Lea Cl. SN25: Swin 5B 12
Leamington Gro. SN3: Swin 6F 29
Lechlade Rd. SN6: High 4F 9
Leicester St. SN1: Swin 4G 5 (2E 29)
Leigh Rd. SN2: Swin 2C 20
Leighton Av. SN3: Swin 4G 29
Lennox Dr. SN3: Swin 2F 29
Lesley Ann Skeete Ct. SN3: Swin 1H 29
Lesley Ct. SN1: Swin 6D 4 (3C 28)
Leslie Cl. SN5: Swin 4D 26
Lethbridge Rd. SN1: Swin 5D 28
Letterage Rd. SN5: Swin 4D 18
Leven SN5: Swin 5D 26
Leverton Ga. SN3: Swin 1G 33
Lewis Cl. SN25: Swin 6A 12
Lewisham Cl. SN25: Swin 3A 20
Lichen Cl. SN2: Swin 2G 19
LIDDINGTON 3G 35
Liddington St. SN2: Swin 3D 20
LIDEN 5C 30
Lidenbrook SN4: Lidd 3G 35
Liden Cen. SN3: Swin 5C 30
Liden Dr. SN3: Swin 5B 30
Lilac Cl. SN2: Swin 4C 20
Lilian Lock Gdns. SN2: Swin 1D 20
Lillybrook SN15: Lyne 1B 36
Lilypad St. SN3: Stra S 6A 22
Lime Cl. SN15: Lyne 3G 37
Lime Kiln SN4: Woot B 2C 24
Lime Kiln Sports Cen. 2C 24
Limes Av. SN2: Swin 3C 20
Lincoln St. SN1: Swin 4F 5 (2D 28)
Linden Av. SN2: Swin 3D 20
Linden Cl. SN4: Woot B 2D 24
Linden Ct. SN1: Swin 3D 4
Linden Way SN5: Swin 4D 18
Lindisfarne SN4: Woot B 2F 25
Lineacre Cl. SN5: Swin 4C 26
Link Av. SN5: Swin 3E 27
Link Cen., The 3E 27
Linley Cl. SN1: Swin 6D 28
Linley Rd. SN26: Blun 3D 12
Linnetsdene SN3: Swin 6B 22
(not continuous)
Linslade Rdbt. SN2: Swin 2A 4 (2B 28)
Linslade St. SN2: Swin 3A 4 (2A 28)
Liskeard Way SN5: Swin 4E 27
Lisle Cl. SN5: Swin 3D 26
Lismore Rd. SN6: High 4D 8
Lister Rd. SN4: Wro 3C 32
Little Av. SN3: Swin 5B 20
Littlecote Cl. SN3: Swin 3G 29

LITTLECOTT 6G 37
Little London SN1: Swin 6G 5 (4E 29)
Lit. London Ct. SN1: Swin 4E 29
(off Little London)
Lit. Park Cl. SN15: Lyne 4D 36
Locksgreen Cres. SN25: Swin 2H 19
Locks La. SN5: Pur 4B 10
Logan Cl. SN3: Swin 2F 29
Lombard Ct. SN5: Swin 4E 27
(off Westminster Rd.)
Lomond Cl. SN5: Swin 4E 19
London St. SN1: Swin 3C 4 (2C 28)
Long Acre SN5: Pur 5B 10
Longcot Cl. SN3: Stra S 5H 21
Longcot Rd. SN6: Shriv, Long 6F 17
Longfellow Cl. SN25: Swin 4B 12
Longfellow Cres. SN4: Woot B 2E 25
Longleat Gdns. SN2: Swin 2D 20
Longleaze SN4: Woot B 2C 24
Longstock Ct. SN5: Swin 2E 27
Longthorpe Cl. SN5: Swin 4G 27
Longworth Dr. SN25: Swin 5F 11
Lonsdale Cl. SN26: Blun 3D 12
Lorne St. SN1: Swin 5B 4 (3B 28)
Lotmead Bus. Pk. SN4: Wan 6E 23
Loughborough Cl. SN5: Swin 6A 12
Louviers Way SN1: Swin 6D 28
Loveage Cl. SN2: Swin 1C 30
Lovell Cl. SN3: Swin 1C 30
Loveridge Cl. SN2: Swin 6F 13
LOWER STRATTON 3H 21
LOWER VILLAGE 1C 12
LOWER WANBOROUGH 4G 31
Lowes Cl. SN5: Swin 4E 19
Loxley Wlk. SN3: Swin 5A 30
Lucas Cl. SN25: Swin 5A 12
Lucerne Cl. SN4: Woot B 1C 24
SN5: Swin 6C 18
Luddesdown Rd. SN5: Swin 4F 27
Ludgershall Rd. SN5: Swin 4A 32
Ludlow Cl. SN3: Swin 4F 29
Lulworth Rd. SN25: Swin 3H 19
Lumley Cl. SN5: Swin 4D 26
Luna Cl. SN25: Swin 5E 11
Lupin Ct. SN2: Stra S 3F 21
Lutyens Ga. SN3: Swin 1G 33
Lyall Cl. SN25: Blun 4A 12
Lyddon Way SN25: Swin 2A 20
Lydford Cl. SN5: Swin 6D 18
Lydiard Country Pk. 2B 26
Lydiard Country Pk. Vis. Cen. 2B 26
Lydiard Flds. SN5: Swin 5B 26
Lydiard House 2B 26
LYDIARD MILLICENT 6A 18
LYDIARD TREGOZE 2C 26
Lyme Way SN5: Swin 1B 20
Lynch Fld., The SN4: Wan 6G 31
Lyndhurst Cres. SN3: Swin 3H 29
LYNEHAM 3F 37
Lyneham Cl. SN2: Swin 6C 12
Lynmouth Rd. SN2: Swin 4A 4 (2A 28)
Lynton Rd. SN2: Swin 5H 19
Lynwood Gro. SN2: Swin 3G 19
Lytchett Way SN3: Swin 2B 30

M

Mackenzie Cl. SN3: Swin 4C 30
Magdalen Rd. SN4: Wan 5G 31
Magic Rdbt., The SN1: Swin 3H 5 (1E 29)
Magnolia Cl. SN2: Swin 4C 20
Magpie La. SN3: Swin 2D 30
Maida Va. SN25: Swin 6G 11
Maiden's Cl. SN6: Watch 3G 17
Maidstone Rd. SN1: Swin 6D 4 (4C 28)
Main Dr. SN25: Blun 4A 12
Main Rd. SN15: Daun L, Lyne 1A 36
Maitland Rd. SN3: Swin 1H 29
Majestic Cl. SN5: Swin 1D 26
Majors Rd. SN6: Watch 2G 17
Maldwyn Cl. SN5: Swin 1C 26
Mall, The SN1: Swin 4C 28
SN6: Shriv 5G 17
Mallard Av. SN15: Lyne 4F 37
Mallard Cl. SN3: Swin 2D 30
Mallow Cl. SN2: Swin 4C 20
Malmesbury Rd. SN4: Woot B 1D 24
SN6: Crick, Leigh 5A 6
Malthouse Cl. SN26: Blun 2D 12
Maltings, The SN4: Wan 5H 31
SN4: Woot B 4C 24

Malvern Rd. SN2: Swin 5D 20
Manchester Rd. SN1: Swin 2E 5 (1D 28)
MANNINGTON 4H 27
Mannington La. SN5: Swin 3G 27
Mannington Pk. SN5: Swin 1A 28
Mannington Retail Pk. SN5: Swin 4H 27
Mannington Rdbt. SN5: Swin 3H 27
Manor Cl. SN4: Wro 5C 32
SN6: Shriv 5E 17
SN26: Blun 2D 12
Manor Cotts. SN3: S Mars 2E 23
Manor Cres. SN2: Swin 4A 20
Manor Gdns. SN2: Swin 5A 20
Manor Ho. Cl. SN4: Woot B 2C 24
Manor La. SN6: Shriv 6E 17
Manor Mdws. SN3: S Mars 2D 22
Manor Orchard SN4: Wan 5H 31
SN6: Crick 2F 7
Manor Pk. SN3: S Mars 2D 22
Manor Rd. SN1: Swin 6A 4 (3A 28)
Manor Vw. SN4: Chi 6B 34
SN4: Lidd 3G 35
Manton St. SN2: Swin 1A 4 (1A 28)
Maple Cl. SN3: Swin 4E 21
Maple Dr. SN4: Woot B 2C 24
Maple Gro. SN2: Swin 4D 20
Marbeck Cl. SN25: Swin 5H 11
March Cl. SN25: Swin 6B 12
Mardale Cl. SN5: Swin 5C 18
Margaret Leckie Ct. SN3: Swin 2F 29
Margaret Matthews Ct. SN2: Swin 1H 27
Marigold Cl. SN2: Swin 2G 19
Marine Cl. SN4: Wro 3C 32
Mariner Rd. SN5: Swin 5E 11
Marjoram Cl. SN2: Swin 1G 19
Markenfield SN5: Swin 4G 27
(not continuous)
Market St. SN1: Swin 4D 4 (2C 28)
Markham Cl. SN3: Swin 1G 29
Markham Pl. SN4: Wro 4A 32
Markham Rd. SN4: Wro 5B 32
Marlborough Cl. SN4: Woot B 2E 25
Marlborough La. SN5: Swin 5E 29
Marlborough Rd. SN3: Swin 5E 29
(not continuous)
SN4: Bad, Chi 4D 34
SN4: Woot B 5C 24
SN4: Wro 4C 32
Marlborough St. SN1: Swin 5B 4 (3B 28)
Marlowe Av. SN3: Swin 1G 29
Marlowe Way SN4: Woot B 2E 25
Marney Rd. SN5: Swin 3D 26
Marsh, The SN4: Wan 6E 31
Marshall Rd. SN5: Swin 6E 19
Marsh Farm La. SN1: Swin 1F 29
Marshfield Way SN3: Stra S 4H 21
Marshgate SN1: Swin 6G 21
Marsland Rd. SN2: Swin 3E 21
Marston Av. SN2: Swin 2E 21
Marston Ga. SN3: S Mars 6B 14
Martens Cl. SN6: Shriv 6D 16
Martens Rd. SN6: Shriv 6E 17
Martinfield SN3: Swin 1C 30
Maryfield SN1: Swin 5G 5
Masefield SN4: Woot B 2E 25
Masefield Av. SN2: Swin 3F 21
Maskeleyne Way SN4: Wro 3A 32
Maslin Row SN3: Stra S 2H 21
(off Delamere Dr.)
Mason Rd. SN25: Swin 6C 12
Masons, The SN5: Pur 6A 10
Massinger Wlk. SN3: Swin 2G 29
(off Lennox Dr.)
Matley Moor SN3: Swin 6D 30
Maunsell Way SN4: Wro 3A 32
Maxey Cl. SN5: Swin 6E 19
Maxwell St. SN1: Swin 4B 4 (2B 28)
Maybold Cres. SN25: Swin 1G 19
May Cl. SN2: Swin 4D 20
May Fld. SN4: Wan 6G 31
Mayfield Cl. SN3: Swin 1A 30
Mayflower Rd. SN3: Stra S 6A 22
Mayfly Rd. SN25: Blun 5D 10
May's La. SN4: Chi 6C 34
Mazurek Way SN25: Swin 6G 11
Meadow Cl. SN4: Woot B 2D 24
Meadowcroft SN2: Stra S 2F 21
Meadow Rd. SN2: Swin 1H 27
SN6: Watch 2H 17
Meadow Springs SN5: Lyd M 6A 18
Meadowsweet Cl. SN25: Swin 1H 19
Meadow Way SN4: Bad, Lidd 3D 34
Meads Bus. Cen., The SN5: Swin 2G 27

Osborne St. SN2: Swin 6C 20
Osprey Cl. SN3: Swin 2D 30
Osterley Rd. SN25: Swin 6H 11
Otter Way SN4: Woot B 3E 25
Overbrook SN3: Swin 4A 30
Overton Gdns. SN3: Stra S 4A 22
OVERTOWN 6E 33
Overtown Hill SN4: Wro 5D 32
Owl Cl. SN3: Swin 2D 30
Owlets, The SN3: Swin 2D 30
Oxford Gdns. SN1: Swin 4C 28
Oxford Rd. SN3: S Mars, Stra S 5H 21
Oxford Sq. SN6: Watch 3F 17
Oxford St. SN1: Swin 3C 4 (2C 28)

P

Pack Hill SN4: Wan 6E 31
Packington Cl. SN5: Swin 1E 27
Paddington Dr. SN3: Swin 2H 27
Paddock, The SN6: High 5F 9
Paddock Cl. SN25: Swin 1A 20
Paddocks, The SN3: Stra S 4H 21
Padstow Rd. SN2: Swin 3A 28
Pakenham Rd. SN3: Swin 4A 30
Palmers Way SN4: Wan 5G 31
Parade, The SN1: Swin 3D 4 (2C 28)
  SN5: Pur 6A 10
Paradise Path SN6: High 4F 9
Paramount SN1: Swin 4F 5
Parhams Ct. SN4: Woot B 3D 24
Parham Wlk. SN5: Swin 3C 26
Park & Ride
  Copse 6E 13
  Wroughton 1D 32
Park Av. SN6: High 5F 9
  SN6: Shriv 6G 17
Park Farm SN25: Swin 3H 19
Park Gdns. SN6: Crick 3E 7
Parklands Rd. SN3: Swin 6H 5 (3F 29)
Park La. SN1: Swin 4A 4 (2B 28)
  SN5: Lyd M 6A 18
PARK NORTH 3H 29
Parkside SN3: Stra S 3H 21
  SN5: Pur 2A 18
PARK SOUTH 4H 29
Park Springs SN5: Swin 3F 27
Parkstone Wlk. SN3: Swin 5A 30
  (off Cranmore Av.)
Park St. SN3: Stra S 4B 22
Park Vw. Dr. SN5: Lyd M 6A 18
Parr Cl. SN5: Swin 2D 26
Parsley Cl. SN2: Swin 1G 19
Parsloes Cl. SN4: Wro 6H 33
Parsonage Ct. SN6: High 4F 9
Parsonage Farm Cl. SN6: Crick 3E 7
Parsonage Rd. SN3: Stra S 3H 21
Parson's La. SN6: Hann 3A 8
Parson's Way SN4: Woot B 4D 24
Partridge Cl. SN3: Swin 2D 30
Passmore Cl. SN3: Swin 1D 30
Pasteur Dr. SN1: Swin 5B 28
Pasture Cl. SN2: Swin 1H 27
Pathfinder Way SN25: Swin 5E 11
Patney Wlk. SN2: Swin 6C 12
Paulet Cl. SN3: Swin 4D 26
Pauls Cft. SN6: Crick 3F 7
Paven Cl. SN5: Pur 5A 10
Pavenhill SN5: Pur 5A 10
Pavenhill Courtyard SN5: Pur 5A 10
Pavilion Cl. SN1: Swin 2H 5 (1F 29)
Paxton Ho. SN1: Swin 4D 28
  (off Prospect Pl.)
Peak, The SN5: Pur 6B 10
Peaks Down SN5: Swin 4E 19
Pearce Cl. SN2: Swin 6F 13
Pearl Rd. SN5: Swin 1C 26
Pear Tree Cl. SN5: Pur 4C 10
PEATMOOR 5D 18
Peatmoor Village Cen. SN5: Swin 5D 18
  (off Shearwood Rd.)
Peatmoor Way SN5: Swin 5D 18
Pembroke Cen. SN2: Swin 5H 19
Pembroke Gdns. SN25: Swin 3H 19
Pembroke Gdns. SN1: Swin 6E 5 (4D 28)
Pencarrow Cl. SN25: Swin 6H 11
Pen Cl. SN25: Swin 2B 20
Pendennis Rd. SN5: Swin 5D 26
Penfold Gdns. SN1: Swin 4D 28
PENHILL 1D 20
Penhill Dr. SN2: Swin 1C 20
Pennine Way SN25: Swin 5A 12

Pennycress Cl. SN25: Swin 2H 19
Pennyhooks La. SN6: Shriv 3D 16
Penny La. SN1: Swin 1G 29
Penrose Wlk. SN3: Swin 3H 27
  (off Dulverton Av.)
Pentridge Cl. SN3: Swin 1B 30
Pentylands Cl. SN6: High 3E 9
Penzance Dr. SN2: Swin 4A 4 (3H 27)
  SN5: Swin 3H 27
Pepperbox Hill SN5: Swin 4E 19
Percheron Cl. SN5: Swin 1D 26
Percy St. SN2: Swin 2A 4 (1A 28)
  (not continuous)
Peregrine Cl. SN3: Swin 6C 22
Periwinkle Cl. SN2: Swin 3F 19
Perry's La. SN4: Wro 4B 32
Peter Furkins Ct. SN1: Swin 5A 4
Petersfield Rd. SN3: Swin 4A 30
Petter Cl. SN4: Wro 3C 32
Pevensey Rdbt. SN5: Swin 4F 27
Pevensey Way SN5: Swin 3F 27
Pewsham Rd. SN2: Swin 1E 21
Pheasant Cl. SN3: Swin 2D 30
Phillips La. SN1: Swin 4E 29
Phobe Way SN25: Swin 5E 11
Phoenix Gdns. SN25: Swin 5E 11
Piccadilly Rdbt. SN3: Swin 1B 30
Pickford Way SN25: Swin 6B 12
Pickwick Cl. SN2: Stra S 1F 21
Picton Rd. SN5: Swin 1D 26
Piernik Cl. SN3: Swin 6H 11
Pigeon Ho. La. SN3: Stra S 3H 21
Pike Ho. Cl. SN6: Crick 2D 6
Pilgrim Cl. SN5: Swin 1D 26
Pilgrims Cl. SN6: Watch 5H 17
Pilton Cl. SN3: Swin 6C 18
Pine Ct. SN2: Swin 4F 21
PINEHURST 3D 20
Pinehurst SN2: Swin 3D 20
Pinehurst Rd. SN2: Swin 5C 20
  (not continuous)
Pinehurst Sports Cen. 3C 20
Pinetree Ri. SN25: Swin 3C 20
Pinnacle, The SN1: Swin 4E 29
Pinnegar Way SN3: Swin 2D 30
Pinnock's Pl. SN2: Stra S 2G 21
Pintail Cl. SN15: Lyne 4F 37
Pioneer Cl. SN5: Swin 1D 26
Pioneer Rd. SN25: Swin 5E 11
Pipers Cl. SN4: Woot B 5C 24
Pipers Rdbt. SN3: Swin 6F 29
Pipers Way SN3: Swin 1D 32
Pipitdene SN3: Swin 1C 30
Pitchens, The SN4: Wro 5C 32
  (not continuous)
Pittsfield SN6: Crick 3E 7
Planks, The SN3: Swin 4E 29
Plattes Cl. SN3: Swin 6E 19
Play Cl. SN5: Pur 5C 10
Plaza, The SN1: Swin 4E 5
Pleydell Rd. SN1: Swin 6D 28
Pleydells SN6: Crick 2E 7
Plummer Cl. SN4: Wro 4B 32
Plymouth St. SN1: Swin 3G 5 (2E 29)
Poachers Way SN25: Swin 5A 12
Polaris Ho. SN2: Swin 1D 4 (1C 28)
Polaris Way SN2: Swin 1D 4 (1C 28)
Polonez Ct. SN25: Swin 6G 11
Poltondale SN3: Swin 1C 30
Pond St. SN25: Swin 1A 20
Pontings Cl. SN26: Blun 2D 12
Ponting St. SN1: Swin 1F 5 (1D 28)
Poole Rd. SN25: Swin 3H 19
Poor St. SN5: Pur 6A 10
Pope Cl. SN25: Swin 1A 20
Poplar Av. SN2: Swin 4D 20
Popplechurch Dr. SN3: Swin 1D 30
Portal Pl. SN15: Lyne 4E 37
Porth Cl. SN25: Swin 5F 11
Portland Av. SN1: Swin 4B 28
Portmore Cl. SN5: Swin 4F 19
Portsmouth St. SN1: Swin 3G 5 (2E 29)
Portwell SN6: Crick 3E 7
Poseidon Cl. SN3: Swin 6E 11
Potterdown Rd. SN2: Swin 1D 20
Poulton St. SN2: Swin 6D 20
Pound Cl. SN15: Lyne 2E 37
Pound La. SN4: Swin 4C 20
Pound Rd. SN6: High 3E 9
Powdrill's Yd. SN3: Stra S 4G 21
Poynings Way SN5: Swin 4C 26
Premier Ho. SN1: Swin 2E 5 (1D 28)

PRESTON 4G 37
Preston La. SN15: Lyne, Pres 3F 37
Primrose Cl. SN3: Swin 1G 19
Primrose Hill SN4: Tock 1H 37
Prince Rupert Ct. SN3: Swin 4D 26
Princess Gdns. SN4: Woot B 3D 24
Princes St. SN1: Swin 3F 5 (2D 28)
PRINNELS, THE 2C 26
Prior's Hill SN3: Wro 5C 32
Priory, The SN6: Crick 1F 7
Priory Grn. SN6: High 4F 9
  (not continuous)
Priory Mnr. SN25: Swin 5H 11
Priory Rd. SN3: Swin 4H 29
Pritchard Cl. SN2: Stra S 1G 21
Prospect Hill SN1: Swin 6F 5 (3D 28)
PROSPECT HOSPICE 4D 32
Prospect Pl. SN1: Swin 6F 5 (4D 28)
Prospero Way SN25: Swin 6G 11
Proud Cl. SN5: Pur 6B 10
PRY, THE 1C 18
Pulsar Rd. SN25: Swin 5E 11
Purbeck Cl. SN3: Swin 1B 30
Purley Av. SN3: Swin 5A 30
Purley Cl. SN4: Wro 4C 32
Purley Rd. SN4: Lidd 1E 35
Purslane Cl. SN3: Swin 3F 19
PURTON 5C 10
Purton Ct. SN5: Pur 5C 10
Purton Mus. 5C 10
Purton Rd. SN2: Swin 4E 19
  SN5: Swin 4D 18
PURTON STOKE 2A 10

Q

Quadrillion Ind. Est. SN5: Swin 1G 27
Quakers La. SN11: Goat 6C 36
Quakers Wlk. SN11: Goat 6D 36
Quarries, The SN1: Swin 5D 28
Quarrybrook Cl. SN3: S Mars 1D 22
Quarry Cres. SN6: High 4E 9
Quarry M. SN1: Swin 5D 28
Quarry Rd. SN1: Swin 4D 28
Queenborough SN5: Swin 4F 27
Queen Elizabeth Dr. SN25: Swin 2F 19
  (not continuous)
Queens Av. SN6: High 3F 9
Queens Dr. SN3: Swin 3H 5 (2F 29)
  (not continuous)
QUEENSFIELD 1E 21
Queensfield SN2: Stra S 1E 21
Queens Rd. SN4: Woot B 3D 24
  SN6: Hann, High 3A 8
Queen St. SN1: Swin 3D 4 (2C 28)
Queintin Rd. SN3: Swin 5E 29

R

Radcot Cl. SN5: Swin 5D 18
Radley Cl. SN3: Swin 1B 30
Radnor St. SN1: Swin 6B 4 (3B 28)
Radstock Av. SN3: Swin 2A 30
Radway Rd. SN3: Stra S 3G 21
RAF Lyneham Airfield 3A 36
Raggett St. SN1: Swin 6E 5 (3D 28)
Raglan Cl. SN3: Swin 6F 29
Rainer Cl. SN3: Stra S 3A 22
Rainham Rd. SN25: Swin 5A 12
Raleigh Av. SN3: Swin 2G 29
RAMLEAZE 2D 26
Ramleaze Dr. SN5: Swin 1D 26
Ramsbury Av. SN2: Swin 1C 20
Ramsden Rd. SN5: Swin 5C 26
Ramsden Rdbt. SN5: Swin 5C 26
Ramsthorn Cl. SN2: Swin 2G 19
Randall Cres. SN6: Swin 6D 18
Randolph Cl. SN3: Swin 3G 29
Rannoch Cl. SN5: Swin 4E 19
Ransome Cl. SN5: Swin 6E 19
Ratcoombe Rd. SN5: Swin 4D 18
Ravenglass Rd. SN5: Swin 2F 27
Ravenscroft SN3: Swin 6B 22
Ravenseft Pk. SN2: Swin 5H 19
Ravens Wlk. SN4: Woot B 3F 25
Rawlings Cl. SN3: S Mars 2D 22
Rawston Cl. SN3: Swin 2B 30
Raybrook Cres. SN2: Swin 2H 27
Ray Cl. SN25: Swin 2B 20
Rayfield Gro. SN2: Swin 6C 20
Reading St. SN1: Swin 3C 4 (2C 28)

Read St.—Shetland Cl.

Read St. SN1: Swin 5B **4** (3B **28**)
Recreation Rd. SN6: Shriv 5E **17**
Rectory Cl. SN4: Wro 6H **33**
Rectory La. SN6: Crick 2F **7**
Redbridge Cl. SN5: Swin 4A **28**
Redcap Gdns. SN5: Swin 1D **26**
Redcliffe St. SN2: Swin 3A **4** (2A **28**)
Redcross Pl. SN1: Swin 6B **4** (3B **28**)
Reddings Ho. *SN3: Swin* *6A* ***22***
(off Twickenham Cl.)
Red Gables Cl. SN5: Pur 6A **10**
Redhouse Gdns. SN25: Swin 5G **11**
Redhouse Way SN25: Swin 5F **11**
REDLANDS 1E **15**
Redlands Cl. SN6: High 6F **9**
Red Lion La. SN6: Crick 2F **7**
Red Lion M. *SN6: High* *4F* ***9***
(off Sheep St.)
Redlynch Cl. SN2: Swin 1D **20**
Redposts Dr. SN5: Swin 4H **27**
Redruth Cl. SN3: Swin 3A **30**
Reeds SN6: Crick 2D **6**
Reema Houses SN6: Seven 3G **15**
Reeves Cl. SN3: Swin 4B **30**
Regent Cir. SN1: Swin 5E **5** (3D **28**)
Regent Cl. SN1: Swin 4E **5** (2D **28**)
Regent Pl. SN1: Swin 4E **5** (2D **28**)
Regents Pl. SN1: Swin 6G **21**
Regent St. SN1: Swin 4D **4** (2C **28**)
Reid's Piece SN5: Pur 6B **10**
Renoir Cl. SN25: Swin 4B **12**
RESTROP 6A **10**
Restrop Rd. SN5: Pur, Rest 6A **10**
Restrop Vw. SN5: Pur 5A **10**
Retingham Way SN3: Stra S 1H **21**
Retreat, The SN6: High 4E **9**
Revell Cl. SN2: Stra S 2F **21**
Reynolds Way SN25: Swin 4B **12**
Rhine Cl. SN5: Swin 4A **28**
Rhuddlan SN5: Swin 4E **27**
Richard Jefferies Gdns. SN4: Chi 6C **34**
Richard Jefferies Mus. 6A **30**
Richards Cl. SN4: Woot B 4C **24**
Richmond Ho. *SN3: Swin* *6A* ***22***
(off Twickenham Cl.)
Richmond Rd. SN2: Swin 5B **20**
Ridge, The SN26: Blun 2C **12**
Ridge Grn. SN5: Swin 1E **27**
Ridge Nether Moor SN3: Swin 6D **30**
Ridgeway, The SN4: Bad, Chi 6D **34**
RIDGEWAY BMI HOSPITAL 4C **32**
Ridgeway Cl. SN2: Swin 4A **20**
Ridgeway Rd. SN2: Stra S 1F **21**
Ridgeway Sports Cen., The 3B **32**
Ridings, The SN2: Swin 6B **20**
Rigel Cl. SN25: Swin 5F **11**
Ringsbury Cl. SN5: Pur 6A **10**
Ringwood Cl. SN3: Swin 2A **30**
Rinsdale Cl. SN5: Swin 5E **19**
Ripley Rd. SN1: Swin 4D **28**
Ripon Way SN3: Swin 5H **29**
Ripple Fld. SN5: Swin 4E **27**
Risingham Mead SN5: Swin 3F **27**
Rivenhall Rd. SN5: Swin 3F **27**
Riverdale Cl. SN1: Swin 6D **28**
Riverdale Wlk. SN1: Swin 6D **28**
Rivergate SN5: Swin 6F **19**
RIVERMEAD 6F **19**
Rivermead Dr. SN5: Swin 6F **19**
Rivermead Ind. Est. SN5: Swin 6F **19**
River Ray Est. SN2: Swin 1G **27**
Rivers Way SN6: High 4E **9**
Roberts Cl. SN4: Wro 5C **32**
Robins Cl. SN4: Woot B 3F **25**
Robinsgreen SN3: Swin 1C **30**
Robinson Cl. SN3: Swin 2C **30**
Roche Cl. SN3: Swin 4C **30**
Rochester Cl. SN5: Swin 4E **27**
Rochford Cl. SN5: Swin 3D **26**
Rockdown Ct. SN2: Swin 2E **21**
RODBOURNE 5A **20**
RODBOURNE CHENEY 3B **20**
Rodbourne Rd. SN2: Swin 1A **4** (6A **20**)
(not continuous)
Rodbourne Rdbt. SN2: Swin 6A **20**
Rodway SN4: Wan 5G **31**
Rodwell Cl. SN3: Swin 4H **29**
Roebuck Cl. SN4: Woot B 3E **25**
Rogers Cl. SN3: Swin 1H **29**
Rolleston St. SN1: Swin 5F **5** (3D **28**)
Roman Cres. SN1: Swin 5C **28**
Roman Wlk. SN6: Watch 2H **17**
Roman Way SN6: High 5E **9**
Romney Way SN5: Swin 2D **26**
Romsey St. SN2: Swin 1A **28**
Rope Yd. SN4: Woot B 4C **24**
Rosary, The SN4: Woot B 3D **24**
Rosebery St. SN1: Swin 1G **5** (1E **29**)
Rose Ct. SN4: Woot B 3D **24**
Rosehill Cl. SN15: Brad 1B **36**
Rosemary Cl. SN2: Swin 1G **19**
Rosendale Rd. SN3: Swin 4A **30**
Rose St. SN2: Swin 1A **28**
Rosetta Cl. SN25: Swin 5E **11**
Rose Wlk. SN25: Swin 1A **20**
Rosewood Ct. *SN3: Swin* *5C* ***30***
(off Liden Dr.)
Ross Gdns. SN3: Stra S 2H **21**
Rother Cl. SN25: Swin 1A **20**
Rotten Row SN4: Wan 5G **31**
ROUGHMOOR 4D **18**
Roughmoor Farm Cl. SN5: Swin 5D **18**
Roughmoor Way SN5: Swin 1D **26**
Roundhills Mead SN6: High 2F **9**
Roundway Down SN5: Swin 5E **27**
Roves Farm Vis. Cen. 6G **15**
Roves La. SN6: Seven 3G **15**
Row, The SN2: Swin 5E **21**
Rowan SN2: Swin 4F **21**
Rowan Dr. SN4: Woot B 4D **24**
Rowan Ho. SN1: Swin 3D **4**
Rowan Rd. SN2: Swin 3B **20**
Rowborough La. SN3: S Mars 3E **23**
Rowland Hill Cl. SN3: Swin 4D **30**
Rowton Heath Way SN5: Swin 4D **26**
Royston Rd. SN3: Swin 4H **29**
Rubens Cl. SN25: Swin 4A **12**
Ruckley Gdns. SN3: Stra S 4A **22**
Rushall Cl. SN2: Swin 1C **20**
Rushmere Path SN25: Swin 1A **20**
Rushton Rd. SN3: Swin 5H **29**
Ruskin Av. SN2: Stra S 3G **21**
Ruskin Dr. SN4: Woot B 2E **25**
Russell Wlk. SN3: Swin 2F **29**
Russley Cl. SN5: Swin 5C **18**
Rutland Rd. SN3: Swin 3G **29**
Ruxley Cl. SN4: Woot B 4C **24**
Ryan Cl. SN5: Swin 4E **19**
Rycote Cl. SN5: Swin 2D **26**
Rydal Cl. SN25: Swin 1A **20**
Rye Cl. SN5: Swin 1D **26**
Rylands Way SN4: Woot B 3D **24**
Rysy Ct. SN25: Swin 6H **11**

S

Sackville Cl. SN3: Swin 1G **29**
Saddleback Rd. SN5: Swin 1D **26**
Sadler Wlk. SN3: Swin 3G **29**
Saffron Cl. SN4: Woot B 1D **24**
SN25: Swin 3H **19**
Sage Cl. SN2: Swin 1G **19**
St Albans Cl. SN2: Swin 1H **27**
St Ambrose Cl. SN3: Swin 2C **30**
St Andrews Cl. SN4: Wro 3C **32**
St Andrews Ct. SN4: Wro 3C **32**
SN25: Blun 4H **11**
St Andrews Grn. SN3: Swin 1D **30**
ST ANDREW'S RIDGE 4B **12**
St Austell Way SN2: Swin 2A **28**
St Clements Ct. *SN3: Swin* *4H* ***29***
(off Horsham Cres.)
St Helens Gdns. SN4: Wro 5C **32**
St Helens Vw. SN1: Swin 4A **28**
St Ives Ct. SN3: Swin 1B **30**
St James Cl. SN2: Stra S 1E **21**
St John Rd. SN4: Wro 3B **32**
St Julians Cl. SN3: S Mars 2D **22**
St Katherine Grn. SN3: Swin 1D **30**
St Margaret Pk. SN3: Stra S 4C **22**
St Margarets Grn. SN3: Stra S 4A **22**
St Margaret's Rd. SN3: Swin 5E **29**
St Marks Tennis Cen. 6D **20**
St Mary's Cl. SN15: Brad 2A **36**
St Mary's Gro. SN2: Swin 6C **20**
St Michaels Av. SN6: High 4D **8**
St Michaels Cl. SN15: Lyne 1D **36**
St Paul's Dr. SN3: Swin 1D **30**
St Paul's St. SN2: Swin 5D **20**
St Phillip's Rd. SN2: Stra S 3F **21**
Salcombe Gro. SN3: Swin 3G **29**
Salisbury St. SN1: Swin 1F **5** (1D **28**)
Salop Cl. SN6: Shriv 6E **17**
Saltash Rd. SN2: Swin 3A **28**
Saltram Cl. SN3: Swin 2B **30**
Salt Spring Dr. SN4: Woot B 4B **24**
Salzgitter Ct. *SN5: Swin* *3F* ***27***
(off Affleck Cl.)
Salzgitter Dr. SN25: Swin 4B **12**
Sams La. SN26: Blun 2D **12**
Sandacre Rd. SN5: Swin 6C **18**
SANDALWOOD COURT 2A **22**
Sandbourne Rd. SN25: Swin 1G **19**
Sandgate SN3: Stra S 5A **22**
Sandgate M. SN3: Stra S 5A **22**
Sand Hill SN6: Shriv 5D **16**
Sandown Av. SN3: Swin 5F **29**
Sandpiper Bri. SN3: Swin 1D **30**
Sandringham Rd. SN3: Swin 5G **29**
Sandstone Rd. SN25: Swin 5A **12**
Sandwood Cl. SN5: Swin 4E **19**
Sandy La. SN1: Swin 4C **28**
SN6: Shriv 6E **17**
Sanford St. SN1: Swin 3E **5** (2D **28**)
Sarsen Cl. SN1: Swin 4A **28**
Savernake Ct. SN1: Swin 6E **5**
Savernake St. SN1: Swin 6D **4** (3D **28**)
Savill Cres. SN4: Wro 3A **32**
Sawyer Rd. SN25: Swin 6C **12**
Saxon Cl. SN6: Crick 3E **7**
Saxon Ct. SN3: Swin 4E **29**
Saxon Mill SN4: Chi 6C **34**
Saxon Orchard SN6: Watch 2G **17**
Saxton Wlk. SN5: Swin 6E **19**
Scarborough Rd. SN2: Swin 6A **20**
Scarlet Cl. SN25: Swin 5A **12**
Scholar Cl. SN6: Watch 5H **17**
School Cl. SN3: Stra S 3A **22**
SN4: Chi 6C **34**
School Row SN25: Swin 2H **19**
Science Mus.
Wroughton 6A **32**
Scimitar Way SN3: Stra S 1A **22**
Scotby Av. SN3: Swin 5F **29**
Scotney Cres. SN25: Swin 6A **12**
Seacole Cres. SN1: Swin 5B **28**
Seagry Ct. SN2: Swin 1C **20**
Seaton Cl. SN25: Swin 1A **20**
Sedgebrook SN3: Swin 6C **30**
Sefton Rd. SN25: Swin 5F **11**
Selby Cres. SN5: Swin 4E **27**
Seldon Cl. SN3: Swin 2F **29**
Semley Wlk. SN2: Swin 2D **20**
Sevenfields SN6: High 3F **9**
SEVENHAMPTON 2G **15**
Severn Av. SN25: Swin 2A **20**
Seymour Rd. SN3: Swin 2G **29**
Shaftesbury Av. SN3: Swin 5A **30**
Shaftesbury Cen. SN2: Swin 2A **4**
Shaftesbury Cl. SN5: Pur 4C **10**
Shakespeare Path SN2: Stra S 3G **21**
Shakespeare Rd. SN4: Woot B 2E **25**
Shalbourne Cl. SN2: Swin 1C **20**
Shanklin Rd. SN25: Swin 2H **19**
Shaplands SN3: Stra S 4H **21**
Shapwick Cl. SN3: Swin 1B **30**
Sharp Cl. SN5: Swin 1E **27**
Shaw Ridge Leisure Pk. 2E **27**
Shaw Rd. SN5: Swin 1E **27**
(Bankfoot Cl.)
SN5: Swin 2F **27**
(The Chesters)
Shaw Village Cen. SN5: Swin 1D **26**
Shearings, The SN1: Swin 4D **28**
Shearwood Rd. SN5: Swin 5D **18**
Sheen Cl. SN5: Swin 4C **26**
Sheep St. SN6: High 4F **9**
Sheerwold Cl. SN3: Stra S 3A **22**
Shelfinch SN5: Swin 4G **27**
Shelley Av. SN4: Woot B 2E **25**
Shelley St. SN1: Swin 5C **4** (3C **28**)
Shenton Cl. SN3: Stra S 3A **22**
Shenton Ct. SN3: Stra S 4A **22**
Shepherds Breach SN4: Woot B 3D **24**
Sheppard St. SN1: Swin 3C **4** (2C **28**)
Shepperton Way SN25: Swin 6B **12**
(Baxter Cl.)
SN25: Swin 6A **12**
(Colbert Pk.)
Sherborne Pl. SN3: Swin 1A **30**
Sherfields SN4: Woot B 4E **25**
Sherford Rd. SN25: Swin 2H **19**
Sheridan Dr. SN4: Woot B 2E **25**
Sheringham Ct. *SN3: Swin* *5C* ***30***
(off Liden Dr.)
Sherston Av. SN2: Swin 1D **20**
Sherwood Rd. SN3: Swin 4A **30**
Shetland Cl. SN5: Swin 1D **26**

Shield Dr.—Teeswater Cl.

Shield Dr. SN15: Lyne 4E 37
Shipley Dr. SN25: Swin 6A 12
Shipton Gro. SN3: Swin 3F 29
Shire Cl. SN5: Swin 1D 26
Shire Ct. SN1: Swin 6A 4 (3B 28)
Shirley Cl. SN3: Swin 1G 29
Short St. SN6: Watch 3G 17
Shoscombe Grn. SN3: Swin 2A 30
Showfield SN4: Woot B 2C 24
Shrewsbury Rd. SN3: Swin 2G 29
Shrewton Wlk. SN2: Swin 6D 12
SHRIVENHAM 6E 17
Shrivenham Hundred Bus. Pk.
SN6: Watch 2F 17
Shrivenham Rd. SN1: Swin 3H 5 (1F 29)
(not continuous)
SN3: S Mars 4D 22
SN6: High 5F 9
SN6: S Mars 4D 22
Shropshire Cl. SN5: Swin 1E 27
Shute Av. SN6: Watch 4G 17
Sidney Cl. SN3: Swin 2F 29
SN5: Swin 4C 26
Sigerson Rd. SN25: Swin 1F 19
Signal Way SN3: Swin 5E 29
Silbury M. SN25: Swin 3H 19
Silchester Way SN5: Swin 2F 27
Silto Ct. SN2: Swin 5A 20
Silverton Rd. SN3: Swin 2A 30
Simnel Cl. SN5: Swin 3C 26
Skewbridge Cl. SN4: Woot B 4B 24
Skinner's Cl. SN6: Hann 3A 8
Skye Cl. SN6: High 3E 9
Slade Dr. SN3: Stra S 6H 21
(not continuous)
Slate Mdw. SN4: Wan 5G 31
Sleaford Cl. SN5: Swin 2D 26
Slessor Rd. SN15: Lyne 4E 37
Slipper La. SN4: Chi 6C 34
Smitan Brook SN3: Swin 2C 30
Snapps Cl. SN4: Wro 5C 32
Snodshill Rdbt. SN3: Swin 5B 30
Snowdon Pl. SN2: Stra S 2F 21
Snowdrop Cl. SN25: Swin 1G 19
Snowshill Cl. SN25: Swin 1A 20
Somerdale Cl. SN5: Swin 2F 27
Somerford Cl. SN2: Swin 2E 21
Somerset Ct. SN4: Wan 5H 31
Somerset Rd. SN2: Swin 5A 20
Somerville Rd. SN3: Swin 2G 29
Sophia Ho. *SN3: Swin 6A 22*
(off Twickenham Cl.)
Sorrel Cl. SN4: Woot B 1D 24
Sound Copse SN5: Swin 4E 19
Southampton St. SN1: Swin 4G 5 (2E 29)
Southbank Glen SN4: Woot B 3E 25
Southbrook St. SN2: Swin 6C 20
Southbrook St. Extension SN2: Swin 5C 20
Southdown SN4: Wan 6G 31
South Dr. SN25: Blun 4A 12
Southernwood Dr. SN2: Swin 2F 19
Southey Cl. SN25: Swin 4A 12
SOUTH MARSTON 1D 22
Sth. Marston Ind. Est. SN3: S Mars 6B 14
South Mdw. La. SN6: Pur S 1B 10
SN26: Pur S 1B 10
South St. SN1: Swin 6F 5 (4D 28)
SN6: Watch 3G 17
Southview SN15: Lyne 1E 37
South Vw. Av. SN3: Swin 3F 29
Southwick Av. SN2: Swin 1C 20
Southwold Cl. SN25: Swin 6E 11
Soyuz Cres. SN25: Swin 5E 11
Spa Cl. SN6: High 3G 9
SPARCELLS 4E 19
Sparcells Dr. SN5: Swin 4E 19
Sparrows La. SN4: Woot B 3C 24
Speedwell Cl. SN25: Swin 1H 19
Spencer Cl. SN5: Swin 1C 26
Spencers Orchard SN4: Wro 4B 32
Spenser Cl. SN3: Swin 1H 29
Speresholt SN5: Swin 4G 27
Spindle Tree Ct. SN2: Swin 4C 20
Spinney Cl. SN4: Lidd 3G 35
Spital La. SN6: Crick 3F 7
Spitfire Way SN3: S Mars 5B 14
Spittleborough Rdbt. SN4: Woot B 6B 26
Spode Cl. SN25: Swin 5G 11
Sprats Barn Cres. SN4: Woot B 3C 24
Spring Cl. SN1: Swin 3F 5 (2D 28)
Springfield Cl. SN6: Shriv 6E 17
Springfield Cres. SN4: Woot B 3C 24
Springfield Rd. SN1: Swin 5D 28
Spring Gdns. SN1: Swin 4F 5 (2D 28)
Spring Gdns. Rdbt. SN1: Swin 3F 5 (2D 28)
Springhill Cl. SN5: Swin 3F 27
Springlines SN4: Wan 5H 31
Spruce Ct. *SN2: Swin 4C 20*
(off Tree Courts Rd.)
Spur Way SN2: Stra S 3F 21
Square, The SN1: Swin 4E 29
Squires Copse SN5: Swin 5D 18
Squires Hill Cl. SN4: Woot B 3E 25
Squires Rd. SN6: Watch 3G 17
Squirrel Cres. SN4: Woot B 3E 25
Stable Ct. SN4: Woot B 3C 24
Stacey's La. SN4: Wan 6H 31
Stackpole Cres. SN25: Swin 4F 11
Stafford St. SN1: Swin 6D 4 (3C 28)
Stainswick La. SN6: Shriv 6F 17
Stallpits La. SN6: Shriv 5C 16
Stallpits Rd. SN6: Shriv 5D 16
Stamford Cl. SN5: Swin 3E 27
Stanbridge Pk. SN5: Swin 1D 26
Stancombe Pk. SN5: Swin 3G 27
Standen Way SN25: Swin 5B 12
Standings Cl. SN5: Swin 6D 18
Stanford Rd. SN25: Swin 5F 11
Stanier St. SN1: Swin 5D 4 (3C 28)
Stanley Cl. SN4: Wan 5G 31
Stanley Honey Ct. SN3: Swin 2G 29
Stanley St. SN1: Swin 6F 5 (3D 28)
Stanmore St. SN1: Swin 6B 4 (3B 28)
Stansfield Cl. SN5: Swin 4G 27
Stanton Ct. SN3: S Mars 5B 14
STANTON FITZWARREN 2A 14
Stanway Cl. SN3: Swin 4H 29
Stapleford Cl. SN2: Swin 6C 12
Stapleford Way SN2: Swin 6C 12
Stapler's La. SN6: Hann 5A 8
Stapleton Cl. SN6: High 5E 9
Stardust Cres. SN25: Swin 5D 10
Staring Cl. SN5: Swin 6C 18
Star La. SN6: Watch 3F 17
Star West SN5: Swin 1G 27
Station App. SN1: Swin 5E 29
Station Ind. Est. SN1: Swin 3C 4 (2C 28)
Station Rd. SN1: Swin 2D 4 (1C 28)
SN4: Chi 6C 34
SN4: Woot B 4C 24
SN5: Pur, Wid 5C 10
SN6: High 4E 9
SN6: Shriv 6E 17
Station Yd. SN5: Wid 4C 10
Staverton Way SN2: Swin 6D 12
Steadings, The SN4: Woot B 4E 25
Stedham Wlk. SN3: Swin 4A 30
Stenbury Cl. SN25: Swin 5B 12
Stenness Cl. SN5: Swin 4F 19
Stephenson Rd. SN25: Swin 5D 12
Stephens Rd. SN3: Stra S 5H 21
Stevenson Rd. SN25: Swin 1F 19
Stewart Cl. SN25: Swin 6C 12
Stinsford Cres. SN25: Swin 6F 11
Stirling Cl. SN4: Wro 3B 32
Stirling Rd. SN3: S Mars 6B 14
Stockbridge Copse SN5: Swin 4E 19
Stockham Cl. SN6: Crick 2F 7
Stockton Rd. SN2: Swin 2D 20
Stoke Comn. La. SN5: Pur S 2A 10
Stokesay Dr. SN5: Swin 4F 27
Stonecrop Way SN25: Swin 1H 19
Stonefield Cl. SN5: Swin 1F 27
SN6: Shriv 6F 17
Stonefield Dr. SN6: High 6F 9
Stonehill Grn. SN5: Swin 2G 27
(not continuous)
Stonehurst Cl. SN3: Stra S 5H 21
Stone La. SN5: Lyd M 5A 18
Stoneover La. SN4: Woot B 3E 25
Stones La. SN6: Crick 1B 6
Stoneybeck Cl. SN5: Swin 2G 27
Stour Rd. SN25: Swin 2C 20
Stour Wlk. SN25: Swin 2C 20
Stranks Cl. SN6: High 6F 9
Stratford Cl. SN5: Swin 3G 27
Stratton Ct. SN3: Stra S 3H 21
SN5: Pur 5B 10
STRATTON GREEN 5A 22
Stratton Orchard SN3: Stra S 4H 21
Stratton Rd. SN1: Swin 6G 21
SN3: Swin 6G 21
STRATTON ST MARGARET 3A 22
Stratton St Margaret By-Pass SN3: Stra S 1H 21
SN3: Swin 6D 30
SN25: Swin 5E 13
Street, The SN4: Lidd 3G 35
SN5: Lyd M 6A 18
SN25: Swin 3H 19
(not continuous)
Stroma Way SN6: High 3D 8
Strouds Cl. SN3: Swin 5E 29
Stroud's Hill SN4: Chi 6C 34
Stuart Cl. SN3: Swin 2G 29
Stubsmead SN3: Swin 3B 30
Studio, The SN1: Swin 4G 5
Studland Cl. SN3: Swin 5A 30
Sudeley Way SN5: Swin 3C 26
Suffolk St. SN2: Swin 6D 20
Summerhouse Rd. SN4: Wro 3A 32
Summers St. SN2: Swin 1A 4 (1A 28)
Sunflowers, The SN2: Stra S 3E 21
Sun La. SN4: Wro 5B 32
Sunningdale Rd. SN25: Swin 2D 20
Sunnyside Av. SN1: Swin 6A 4 (4B 28)
Supermarine Rd. SN3: S Mars 4C 14
Supermarine Sports & Social Club 4C 14
Surrey Rd. SN2: Swin 5B 20
Sussex Sq. SN3: Swin 2G 29
Sutton Pk. SN26: Blun 3D 12
Sutton Rd. SN3: Swin 4B 30
Swallowdale SN3: Swin 1C 30
Swallowfield Av. SN3: Swin 3G 29
Swallows Mead SN4: Woot B 3F 25
Swanage Wlk. SN25: Swin 3H 19
SWANBOROUGH 6B 8
Swanbrook SN3: Swin 6C 22
Swan Cl. SN3: Stra S 6A 22
Swift Av. SN25: Swin 5B 12
Swinburne Pl. SN4: Woot B 2D 24
SWINDON 4D 4 (2C 28)
Swindon and Cricklade Railway
Hayes Knoll Station 2C 10
(Tadpole La.)
Swindon Arts Cen. 4E 29
Swindon Europark SN5: Swin 6E 27
Swindon Mus. & Art Gallery *4D 28*
(off Bath Rd.)
SWINDON NEW TOWN 4E 5 (2D 28)
Swindon Rd. SN1: Swin 6E 5 (3D 28)
SN3: Stan F 4C 14
SN3: Stra S 5H 21
SN4: Woot B 1E 25
SN4: Wro 3C 32
SN6: Calc, Crick 3G 7
SN6: High, Stan F 4C 14
Swindon Stadium (Greyhound & Speedway) 4B 12
Swindon Station (Rail) 2D 4 (1C 28)
Swindon St. SN6: High 5F 9
Swindon Town FC 2H 5 (1E 29)
Swinley Dr. SN5: Swin 4D 18
Sword Gdns. SN5: Swin 4A 28
Sycamore Cl. SN15: Lyne 3G 37
Sycamore Gro. SN2: Swin 4D 20
Symonds SN5: Swin 5E 27
Syon Cl. SN25: Swin 6A 12
Sywell Rd. SN3: Stra S 6B 22

T

Tadpole La. SN25: Blun 4D 10
Tallis Wlk. SN5: Swin 3D 26
Tallow La. SN4: Wan 5G 31
Tamar Cl. SN25: Swin 2B 20
Tamworth Dr. SN5: Swin 1D 26
Tanners Cl. SN4: Woot B 3C 24
Tansley Moor SN3: Swin 5D 30
Taplow Wlk. SN3: Swin 4H 29
Tarka Cl. SN25: Swin 5A 12
Tarragon Cl. SN2: Swin 2F 19
Tatley Wlk. SN4: Chi 6D 34
Tatry Rd. SN25: Swin 6G 11
Tattershall SN5: Swin 5F 27
Taunton St. SN1: Swin 4B 4 (2B 28)
Tavistock Rd. SN3: Swin 2A 30
TAW HILL 1F 19
Tawny Owl Cl. SN3: Stra S 6B 22
Taylor Cres. SN3: Stra S 2H 21
Teal Av. SN15: Lyne 3E 37
Tealsbrook SN3: Swin 1C 30
Techno Trad. Est. SN2: Swin 5E 21
(Athena Av.)
SN2: Swin 5F 21
(Bramble Rd.)
Tedder Cl. SN2: Swin 4C 20
Tees Cl. SN25: Swin 2B 20
Teeswater Cl. SN5: Swin 2D 26

50 A-Z Swindon

The representation on the maps of a road, track or footpath is no evidence of the existence of a right of way.

The Grid on this map is the National Grid taken from Ordnance Survey® mapping with the permission of the Controller of Her Majesty's Stationery Office.

SAFETY CAMERA INFORMATION

Safety camera locations are publicised by the Safer Roads Partnership who operate them in order to encourage drivers to comply with speed limits at these sites. It is the driver's absolute responsibility to be aware of and to adhere to speed limits at all times.

By showing this safety camera information it is the intention of Geographers' A-Z Map Company Ltd., to encourage safe driving and greater awareness of speed limits and vehicle speed. Data accurate at time of printing.

Printed and bound in the United Kingdom by Gemini Press Ltd., Shoreham-by-Sea, West Sussex
Printed on materials from a sustainable source